WHAT PEOPLE AR

THE WAY O1

Luitha has walked the shaman's path for many years and now invites you to experience self-empowerment through *The Way of Change*. Overflowing with down-to-earth guidance and exercises, this book shows you not only how you can effect change in your life but also how you can grow in the process – connecting to nature, learning your truth, finding your courage, and touching your sacred self. Heartfelt, compassionate, and deeply practical, Luitha's book is a wonderful guide to have by your side.

Mike Williams, author of *Follow the Shaman's Call: An Ancient Path for Modern Lives*

Change is going to happen – so it's better to approach it with grace and welcome... and this book points the way to achieving this. Easily acessible, well written and heartful.

Nick Wood, Sacred Hoop Magazine

I loved this book – it was so packed full of exercises and practical things to try it was almost too much! I loved how relatable to daily life it was and how down to earth too – a very approachable introduction to some of the shaman ways.

Lea Woodward, Location Independent

The simplistic act of ceremony has been captured beautifully in *The Way of Change*. Reconnecting to the sacred in all things has been brought to life in this lovely book.

Julie Dollman, Shaman and owner of Ayni Shamans Shop, Author of *Living Shamanism*

The Way of Change

Finding Your Power to Thrive in a Changing World

The Way
of Change

Finding Your Power to Thrive in
a Changing World

Luitha K. Tamaya

AXIS MUNDI
BOOKS

Winchester, UK
Washington, USA

First published by Axis Mundi Books, 2013
Axis Mundi Books is an imprint of John Hunt Publishing Ltd., Laurel House, Station Approach,
Alresford, Hants, SO24 9JH, UK
office1@jhpbooks.net
www.johnhuntpublishing.com
www.axismundi-books.com

For distributor details and how to order please visit the 'Ordering' section on our website.

Text copyright: Luitha K. Tamaya 2012

ISBN: 978 1 84694 959 3

A CIP catalogue record for this book is available from the British Library.

Design: Stuart Davies

Printed and bound by CPI Group (UK) Ltd, Croydon, CR0 4YY

We operate a distinctive and ethical publishing philosophy in all
areas of our business, from our global network of authors to
production and worldwide distribution.

CONTENTS

Preface

I wrote this book because I believe in the power of change, and in our power to dance through the transformations of our lives with grace and vision. Change is a two-way gift; it allows us to learn about and practice our deepest, most empowering, healed natures and then gives us the opportunities to re-create the world how we'd really like it to be, every single day.

I've personally experienced huge amounts of change, both beautiful and painful, over the years of my shamanic training as well as before I began walking this path, ranging from divorce, chronic illness and homelessness, to close encounters with death and the miracle of healing through the grace of Spirit. Each and every change that I've ever encountered has taught me something; each wonderful gift from each wonderful transition has become, in the traditional way of the shaman, my medicine – the power that I bring to the world.

But change and it's gifts aren't just for medicine people and healers – we can all work with and benefit from the power of change in our lives. After all, we all have to live with change on a daily basis, so we all know it very well and have plenty of chances to discover it's medicine!

This book is offered as a map for how we can all work with change, and it includes the various powerful practices that I've used when dealing with change, both as a shaman and simply as a human being who lives in a constantly changing world.

The practices can be used by anyone, and I've made them as accessible and open to interpretation as possible without losing their power, because I believe that everyone has a unique and equally valuable approach to their own personal growth, healing and relationship with the Sacred.

Working with that uniqueness is what makes spiritual paths both so challenging and so valuable, and I encourage everyone who reads this book to honour it within them as they work through the practices.

This book would never have been written without the web of support and encouragement woven by my guides, teachers and most especially my husband; thank you all for teaching me everyday about the power that lives within us all, and for walking this path beside me.

And thank you too, for having the courage and vision to look at change in a new way. May we all learn to thrive in this changing world, and, so doing, to dream it anew together each and every day, more and more beautifully.

Blessings on your journey with this book,

Luitha Tamaya

email: luitha@thelivingsacred.org
www.lktamaya.co.uk

Section One:

All About Change

Those who give themselves to Wakan-Tanka discover that
every winter of life is followed by spring.
Fools Crow

Why Change?

Change is the process of transformation from one state to another. The movement of the sun from the East to the West each day is a process of change – of transformation from one position to another. Journeys are all processes of change; we begin in one state or place, and end in another: change is the transition between those two states.

So when we think about it, life is, essentially, a process of constant change; from birth to adulthood to death. Every day that we live, we are engaged in this process of living transformation, as well as many, many other transitions, journeys, processes and changes.

We are surrounded by change every day. The sun comes up and then falls, our children learn and grow, our bodies age, our minds experience new things and so mature. Our societies change their structures, their governments and their values. Countries rise and fall in prosperity and peace. The seasons cycle, the weather is forever moving and our ecosystems shift, adapt and even sometimes collapse. The years turn, people are born and die, and even our roles, beliefs and relationships end. The very act of breathing is itself a process of change - we are beings of change by our very nature.

So to be alive in this world is to be constantly surrounded, both within and without, by change. Even when we die we don't really stop changing - our bodies will undergo a process of transformation back into the cycle of change as food, soil, air, and water.

Looking at change in this way, it becomes clear that if we aren't comfortable with change, we aren't really comfortable with being alive at all. And yet, so many of us have problems with change. From death to economic fluctuations to relationship changes, we all avoid looking at the reality that change is only a moment away – like when we won't talk about the possibility of old age, retirement, death or divorce. We become frozen in fear at the thought of the changes that could happen, might happen, probably will happen, and even those that definitely will happen. And if we are not comfortable with change, we certainly cannot be truly comfortable in our lives, or with ourselves.

When we are avoiding or worrying about the changes that are going on around us, we are at a huge disadvantage. It takes a huge amount of energy to avoid looking at change, and to repress the emotions we're feeling about the changes around us. This is energy that could otherwise be used for our well being – creating what we want in our lives, healing old issues or wounds, building loving relationships and generally enjoying our lives. But when we can't face change this energy is stagnated or blocked, leaving us tired, ill or depressed, and even making us physically ill.

And on top of this loss of energy and vitality, we can miss all of the great opportunities that change offers to us; all the doorways that are opened when one thing ends and another begins, all the ideas and new avenues we could be exploring, avenues that could hold amazing, healing, joyful discoveries. All of these treasures go to waste when we're too afraid to look for them in the shifting reality around us.

And fear itself leaves us crippled, no longer free to choose how to live our lives. From stress at the changes in our work environment and economy, to worry at the changes in our families and children, to panic at the changes in international structures and countries, to downright terror in the face of our own, inner change, like spiritual growth, challenges to our beliefs, accepted truths and values, ageing and our eventual deaths. We become frozen, unable to make full use of our personal power or to even enjoy what we're experiencing right now.

Learning to be truly alive means learning how to be with change; how to relate to it, and ultimately how to thrive with it.

Fortunately, our relationship with change is something that we can all work on. This is a personal process, one that we can do only for ourselves and no one else, and it involves working on four aspects or powers that we all have: Connection, Truth, Courage and Vision.

This book aims to help you work with these powers, enabling you to positively transform your relationship with change so that you can live a more joyful, empowered and fulfilled life. Each of the four main sections describes one of these powers, and gives practices for their cultivation.

Connection and **Truth** give us still places in which to stand when all else about us is in chaos. Through having a personal relationship with that which is unchanging, and by knowing who we are and what is most important to us, we need never fear becoming lost as we go through the changes of life.

Courage allows us to maintain the practices that will help us to thrive, as well as freeing us to make the best choices for our well-being. Having courage means that we are able to listen to the inner wisdom of our hearts, and that we are then more likely to put that wisdom into practice. And being able to engage consciously with change means taking responsibility for ourselves and our lives, something that requires a great deal of courage.

And lastly, **Vision** is the ability to perceive clearly - to see what is, what could be, and what we'd like to be. When we have vision we no longer have to accept other people's interpretations of our lives, but can choose for ourselves what is possible. Being able to see the opportunities before us, as well as the outcomes that we'd like, allows us to fully participate in the changing world; an empowering state to be in, and one that allows us to transform the world that we all live in as we move together into a new era.

Combined, these four powers allow us to relate to change in a totally new way; open, present and peaceful, no matter what.

The Story Of Change

We all have beliefs and habitual ways of thinking about change. Some of these are helpful to us, while other ways of perceiving aren't so helpful any more. Our beliefs and perceptions are like walls around a room – they contain what's possible, what's real, and what's true within a certain set of boundaries. Anything that exists outside of those boundaries is discounted or ignored.

And this can be helpful for us; it certainly is useful to have common, reliable boundaries within which to frame our lives. But sometimes these boundaries can become unhelpful – such as when the reality they describe is no longer healthy for us, but is instead creating pain, fear or any other lack of well being.

This is exactly how it is with change; our old beliefs and patterns of thinking about change can actually hold us where we don't want to be, preventing us from moving on into a more healthy relationship with it. For example, if we were to believe that change is unpredictable, that could foster a sense of tension and fear in us with regards to change and when it could happen in our lives. This, in turn, can reduce the ways that we can respond to the possibility of change, leaving us defensive, unable to take advantage of opportunities as they appear, as well as reducing our enjoyment of the transitions and processes that make up our lives.

Practice: Three Symbol Story

Before we begin to work with our relationship to change, it can be really helpful to know how we currently feel about and perceive change in our lives. When we know what the key issues in this relationship are, we can hold those issues in mind and work with them as we move forward.

A really great way to uncover our fundamental way of seeing something is to tell a story about it. Stories are complex, multi-levelled maps that operate in all the areas of our lives; a story can be taken literally, metaphorically, or can speak to us on a spiritual level that goes beyond words. Because of this, telling our story about something gives us access to a wealth of understanding about our relationship to it; it's because of this that storytelling has been used as a healing tool and spiritual practice since ancient times.

And don't worry – you don't need to be a novelist or a poet to be able to use this powerful tool. Stories are part of us, and when you look around you, you'll realise that stories are everywhere, even now in our modern world. Just think about the programs you watch on TV, the articles you read in newspapers, the books, films and magazines you enjoy – these are all stories.

And we tell stories with each other, every day. Think about how many times you've recounted something that happened during your day to a friend, or how often you've been told the same story by a family member, every time you see them!

These are everyday stories, and while they do reveal a lot about the maps and perception of their tellers, we can use story-telling as an even more powerful tool for personal insight by consciously crafting a mythic story that can hold the wisdom and awareness that we're looking for. A mythic story is one that uses the language of symbolism as well as words, allowing us to access the deeper wisdom of our unconscious. And while this may sound difficult, or imprecise, there is a simple method for creating such a story.

Three symbol stories are a way to tell the mythic story we are currently living. To do this, we use a pack of cards, such as tarot, oracle or contemplation cards; any cards with images on their faces.

Find a quiet place to sit for a while with your cards and your journal. Give yourself permission to take this time out for yourself and take a moment to settle before continuing.

Take two or three slow breaths, releasing all other considerations except what you are doing. Then ask for Spirit or the Sacred to be with you, either silently or out loud, so that you have spiritual support for the work you are about to do.

When you're ready, take your pack of cards and hold them up in front of you. Tell the cards what you're doing by blowing over them, holding in your mind as you do so an image of what you are about to do. Then shuffle the pack and draw three cards, placing them face down in front of you. Put the rest of the pack to one side.

Turn over the cards one by one, taking time to really see their images. Pay no attention to any words on the cards, and instead let the images communicate with you. What details jump out to you? How do they make you feel?

Once you have looked at each card, pick up your journal and pen. You are going to write a story, and the first words of the story are "In a changing world..."

Write the rest of the story, using the cards you picked as the scenes for the beginning, middle and end.

Take only 5 minutes to write, and don't worry about whether it's a good story, or the right one. Just write the first story that comes to you, whatever that may be.

When you have finished writing, thank spirit for being with you and put away your cards and journal. Go back to your day.

A day or two later, take your journal and sit with it for a while. Read your story over a few times, and at least once out loud. Notice how it makes you feel in your body - is it tight, or achy, or light? Do you recognise this story in your life? Who are you in the story? And is this the story that you want to live? How would you like it to end? Are there any parts which make you feel uncomfortable or over which you hesitate when reading?

The answers to these questions will tell you more about how you personally relate to change at the moment, and whether that relationship is working for you or not. They will also give you clues as to how you'd like to relate to change, and how you can go about making those shifts within yourself.

Remember that the story is symbolic; the elements and situations in it represent elements and situations in your life, from the perspective of your soul rather than your mind. Allow these symbols to speak to you; what do they mean to you personally?

For example, you may tell a story about a person who crosses a river to reach their home. The river may represent many things – the flow of time, or of emotions; the lives of the ancestors; the Sacred Feminine in her incarnation as Mother of the Waters. The interpretation that you use will be based on your own, personal experiences and associations, so only you can know what they are. And likewise, as you grow and shift in your relationship with change, these associations and meanings will shift as well as you begin to see the deeper layers of the truth.

The Journey of Change

This book is, in a way, a journey. The practices and exercises in it will take you from where you are now, your current relationship with change, to a more aware, stable one. Through working with these practices and tools, you will explore the four areas of your inner life that can help you become more comfortable with change: your sense of connection, your understanding of truth, your ability to be courageous and your power to envision the world.

If life is a process of change, from beginning to end, then we must accept that any problem with change lies not in the world around us and the changes we experience in it, but in ourselves and how we relate to those changes. We cannot change life and what it means to be alive in this world, but we can change ourselves.

The practices in this book are all designed to develop your ability to thrive in the midst of change - they are going to help you to change yourself, and to feel comfortable doing so.

It is important to mark the beginning of any journey; to envision where we are headed, to ask for guidance and support along the way, and to honour and release where we have come from so that we are free to move on. This book takes you on such a journey, and I highly recommend that you honour your first step on this journey with a ceremony of some sort.

Many spiritual traditions have ceremonies for recognising transitions; they understand that by honouring the changes that we experience in our lives, we can better receive the gifts and wisdom that they offer us, allowing us to move forward in freedom.

Ceremonies are powerful tools for healing and empowerment; through working at a mythic level and letting our minds fall away for a moment, we can access great internal resources as well as the support of the whole universe in our times of transition.

Practice: Ceremony for Change - A Despacho Ceremony

To this end, I invite you to hold a change ceremony, and I have outlined two ceremonies that you could use to do this. Choose whichever one feels right to you, whichever ceremony speaks to you.

And remember that ceremony is a personal, fluid thing - if a part of my outline doesn't work for you, do something else instead. Or even better - make up your own ceremony! What is important is the intent behind the actions, and the symbolism they hold for you.

The Despacho ceremony comes from the Quechuans of South America, and is a way to offer thanks and to bring harmony, or ayni, to your life. There are many types of Despacho ceremony, and they can be used for many purposes. The Ceremony below is the basic ceremony, which you can personalise to your situation and the intent of the ceremony.

To do this ceremony, you will need:

- a piece of paper
- some thread, wool or ribbon
- some offerings to make such as sweeties, chocolate, sugar, seeds, raisins, oats, flower petals, a thimble of red and white wine and anything else that may symbolise what you are offering thanks for – these will hold your gratitude
- three bay leaves or leaves from a plant that you feel connected to, picked with it's permission – these will hold your prayers

1. Collect all of the items you will need in a quiet place where you will not be disturbed. You might like to play some

gentle music, to light a candle, or to meditate for a while before beginning. Take some deep breaths and allow yourself to become centred and still, and then begin the ceremony.

2. Create a sacred space around you by calling out to the four directions of North, South, East and West, and then the Earth and Sky, asking them to hold you as you make your offering. Then, call to Spirit, asking for it to be with you and to guide you in your ceremony. You can also call on any guides, ancestors or teachers that you work with to be present for the ceremony as well.

3. Once you have created the sacred space, place the piece of paper in front of you and fold it into thirds both vertically and horizontally to create a container for your offerings.

4. When you are ready, pick up one of the offerings you prepared, and blow gratitude for one of the blessings in your life into it, filling it with your intent to give thanks. Then put the offering into the centre square of the paper, where ever you feel called to place it.

   Continue to blow your gratitude for the blessings in your life into the offerings, placing them into the centre of your bundle where and how it feels right to you.

5. When you are ready to complete the ceremony, take the three leaves and hold them while you focus again on the gratitude you are feeling for this moment in your life. Into the first leaf, blow all of your appreciation for the blessings and gifts that the past has given you. Then, place the leaf into the bundle, letting go of that old phase of your life as you do so.

   Into the second leaf, blow all of your dreams for the

new phase that is coming into your life now. Give gratitude for the opportunities and gifts this phase will bring you, and then release it to Spirit as you place the leaf into the bundle beside the first.

Into the last leaf, blow all of your gratitude for what never changes; the Sacred and your connection to it, which is always there for you. Place the final leaf into the bundle and take a moment to absorb the beauty of your offering.

6. Fold the rest of the paper over the bundle, being careful to keep all of the offerings inside. Tie the bundle with some thread, red and white is good as it represents the sacred masculine and feminine combined. Wrap your bundle in a piece of cloth, being careful to keep it upright at all times, and then place it somewhere safe and quiet until you are ready to complete the ceremony out in nature.

7. Finally, close the sacred space by thanking each direction for holding your ceremony, and by thanking your ancestors, guides, teachers and Spirit for witnessing your offering of gratitude.

8. To complete the Despacho, you will release the bundle to Spirit, either by placing it in a fire, giving it to running water or the sea, or by burying it in the earth. Create a sacred space, just like when you made your bundle, and let go of your gratitude and prayers as you give the Despacho to the elements and to Spirit for them to transform.

When you are ready, close the sacred space like you did before and know that your prayers have been received.

Practice: Ceremony for Change – Planting a Seed of Change

Whether you have a garden or not, planting a seed or plant as a symbol of the change you want to nurture is a great ceremony for beginning a journey of change. Choose a place that will work well; your windowsill could be perfect, as could the middle of your lawn if you choose.

Choose a plant that will be happy in the space you have picked, either seeds or a young plant that won't be harmed by being moved. The plant might be a species that you already have a relationship with, or it could be a special new type of plant that will represent your relationship with change from now on. Whatever plant and location you choose, just remember that the most important criteria is that it feels good and right to you.

On the day that you plant your seed, go to the place you have chosen and take a moment to remember the reasons you are setting out on this journey. Call for the sacred to be with you and to witness your commitment to come into a good relationship with change.

Tell the sacred and your chosen plant, either silently or out loud, what your intention is. Dig your hole and scatter something biodegradable, such as paper, leaves, flowers or even plant food into the bottom of the hole to represent the old state that you are letting go of. Know that as you do this you are letting go of that old you, thanking it and honouring it for all its help as you do so.

Place your seed or small plant into the hole, holding in your mind the intention that with this plant you are calling in the new state of being that you want to create.

Thank the plant and the earth for their help and support, and fill in the whole gently. Take a few moments to let your actions sink in, and then thank spirit and end the ceremony.

Over the coming weeks, your care for the plant will remind you of the journey you are making, and will nourish you as you make the effort to grow. And if, at any time, you feel lost or confused, or simply need support, you can always go and spend time with your plant.

Section Two:

Connection.

"My place is the Placeless,
My trace is the Traceless,
I am neither body or soul,
for I belong to the soul of the Beloved."
Rumi

Connection is a state of being linked or joined together; the word derives from the Latin connexionem, meaning "a binding or joining together". For example, we can connect pipes or wires, allowing energy, water or information to flow through them from one place to another. We can connect with other people, meaning that we feel somehow touched by another, understanding them and their point of view.

We can have a connection to make – a way of moving forward, travelling or making a journey, such as a flight or train connection. And we can make a connection in our minds, becoming aware of something that was previously lost or unconscious.

All these examples illustrate part of what I mean by connection here; to be linked to something - allowing flow both to and from us; feeling personally touched and having a sense of understanding of what's beyond ourselves; being able to move forward and make our journey; and finding awareness of something we have lost, are all part of having a sense of connection in our lives.

We all long and look for this sense of connection; whether we are making love or playing team sports, making money or raising children, it is part of what defines the human journey.

In relation to change and how we feel about it, connection is an anchor that we can rely on in the midst of the storm; when everything around us is moving and transforming, our sense of connection can be a source of peace and power; something we know we can rely on.

Connection in this way comes from having a personal relationship with what I call the Sacred. By this, I don't necessarily mean a God, Goddess or external being, but the essential nature of creation and reality; for me, with my shamanic training and tradition, I often call the Sacred "Great Spirit", but it has an infinite number of names – as many as there are people relating to it.

The Sacred is what we can all feel beneath the world around us, or beyond it. It exists in the silence that lies behind all sound, and while many people experience it as a sentience or consciousness, many others experience it as an energy, a sense of love, truth or light, with no sense of it being an entity at all.

This is because our relationship with the Sacred is, and can only be, unique and personal. We cannot experience the Sacred through anyone else's life; we see it through our own perspective, in a totally individual way.

So to build a relationship with the Sacred that is real and meaningful to us, we must be able to experience the sacred in our own way, directly and intimately. We cannot build a sense of connection and relationship with the Sacred through reading about, listening to or witnessing other people's experiences; we can learn about how they work with that connection, how they build it and how they experience it, but to actually have that sense of connection in our own lives we have to have that direct experience ourselves.

And personal experience of the Sacred is not something that we can go out and buy - it is a subtle and elusive thing, different for each person. While meditation, or yoga, or communion, or rock climbing might help some people connect, for others it can be music, dance, gardening or cooking. The important thing to understand here is that to have a personal experience of the Sacred you have to be willing to do the things that might help you to connect, and to explore your experiences and preferences so that you can find out what works for you.

While we can't go and buy a personal experience of the Sacred, we can invite the Sacred into our lives and our awareness through actively providing opportunities for it to appear. If we actively welcome the Sacred, creating opportunities and openings for it in our lives and in our minds, it will be there. And one day, we will feel its presence.

Faith – Being Open To Spirit

"Cleave a piece of wood, I am there; lift up the stone and you
will find Me there."
Jesus of Nazareth

The first stage in developing our sense of connection, is to have that first, conscious, experience of it. It can be difficult to access these experiences of the Sacred at first, especially in our materially focused culture. In fact, it is possible to go through our entire lives without feeling this sense of connection, and if we don't take the time to be open to it, it can pass us by.

This is why this section is entitled 'Faith' – faith is the ability to hold a space for the Sacred in our lives, despite never having seen or felt it before. We have to be open to the Sacred without knowing how or when it will appear to us, so that we can experience it personally and directly for ourselves in the way that we need.

One way to describe it is that it's like we go through life with a very old friend, and this friend is always there beside us. But we cannot see them - we are too focused on the outer world, what we're doing and what we are thinking. We have forgotten them.

It is not usually until we decide to sit down and take some time out that we may even remember that our friend exists. But when we do, we begin to look for them, maybe to call for them.

This is the moment when we can finally open our eyes and see them - right beside us, where they've always been.

The Sacred is like that old friend: it cannot force us to pay attention to it and we cannot force ourselves to remember it, or to open our eyes. It is not that the Sacred leaves us, it can't – it's the essence of life itself, so it's always there. It's just that we can forget that it's there, and it's not until we remember and really want to see it, and then give ourselves the opportunities to see it, that we can become aware of its constant presence.

So to begin to have a personal experience of the sacred, we must be willing to try new things and be open to new feelings. And ultimately, we must want to have an experience.

There are so many ways that we can use to create a space for ourselves to open to Spirit, and in the rest of this chapter I've detailed some of the ones that have worked for me. But these aren't the only methods you could use - if none of them ring true for you, or you find that something else might work better, then explore the other methods of connecting that are in this book. Try any ideas that you find, or better yet - make up your own ways to connect with the Sacred by following your own heart and listening to the yearning of your soul.

Practice: Creating Sacred Space

At the heart of building a place for the Sacred in your life is the practice of opening Sacred Space. Sacred Space is simply a defined place and time where the mundane concerns of life can fall away and we can open our eyes to the sacred, safely and in a comfortable, predictable way.

When we open sacred space, we are calling to the Sacred to be with us, and at the same time we're calling for ourselves to be present, to be aware of the space around us and how we're relating with Spirit. It is a way of making the presence of the Sacred conscious so that we can work with it.

There are so many ways of creating Sacred Space, and some of them will be more familiar and comfortable to you than others. Like all the practices I give you, remember to do only what feels right to you and to follow your own instincts about opening sacred space.

Any practice where you call on Spirit or the Sacred to be present with you is a way of opening sacred space. Many people use prayer, silent or out loud, to create their space, while others use ceremony such as lighting a candle or incense, rattling, singing or sitting in silence. The thing to remember is that you're calling on the Sacred to be with you - simply asking Spirit to join you is enough, so long as you mean it.

To open sacred space, choose a place where you won't be disturbed and take a few moments to relax, focusing on your breathing. Let your sense of the normal world fade in your mind as you settle into where you are right now.

Then, using the method you have chosen, reach out to Spirit. Call for it to come, in the way and name that you are most comfortable with. For this first time, simply have the intent that you're establishing this connection consciously in your life and are ready to begin experiencing it for yourself.

Below is a personal prayer that I sometime use to create sacred space, which is similar to the prayers used by various shamans all over the world. Feel free to use it until you find your own, and to modify the wording to suit your own sense of the Sacred.

Opening Prayer

I call to the Spirit of the South,
Come and be with me.
I call to the Spirit of the West,
Come and be with me.
I call to the Spirit of the North,
Come and be with me.
I call to the Spirit of the East,
Come and be with me.
I call to the Spirit of the Earth and of the Sky,
Come and be with me.
I call to the Spirits of my ancestors, my guides and teachers,
Come and be with me.
I call to the Great Spirit,
Come and be with me.

Be open to how you experience the presence of the Sacred,

allowing yourself to feel your own, personal sense of it. Welcome it and thank it for being with you.

When you have finished your practice, close sacred space by thanking Spirit in what ever name or form you used to called it, and then release it, knowing that it will be with you for the rest of the day whether you're aware of it or not.

Practice: Following Your Heart

Think about the things you are most passionate about in your life, whether that's your children, your art, your sport, or your charity. Whatever it is that makes you feel alive, excited and present in the moment. Then notice how thinking about that subject makes you feel in your body - is there a lightness, a buzzing or an opening sensation? Do you feel like laughing, or are you quiet and peaceful? How does your heart feel?

Our passions and love are like channels for Spirit to flow through us. When we fill ourselves with that feeling, maintaining an awareness of the sensations, we often find that what we're really experiencing is a Sacredness, a connection to something greater than ourselves that is giving us that wonderful feeling.

By noticing this feeling, and what elicits it for us, we're taking our first step towards being able to recognise and consciously work with that connection to the Sacred, so these passions and paths of the heart are hugely important to pay attention to. Try journalling about the feelings you notice and when you get them, writing down your answers to the above questions and seeing how they change over time, or between different subjects.

Practice: Being Alone

Spending some time alone is another great way to get a first taste of our connection with the Sacred. You don't need to meditate or visualise anything, simply listen to the world around you and within you. Take some time to just sit and be present without any particular focus, and then call to Spirit to join you. Notice any changes that you feel. Do you still feel alone? How does the space around you feel when you close your eyes? Are you more or less aware of your internal chatter and feelings?

By learning the difference between how you feel when you're on your own in a mundane way, and how you feel when you're alone but focused on Spirit, you can being to recognise how the Sacred feels and affects you, as well as which ways of calling Spirit work for you.

At first, the contrast or difference may be hard to feel, but as you spend more time paying attention to it you will become more aware of the subtle sensations and emotions that accompany your connection.

Practice: Community

Another powerful way of connecting with the Sacred for the first time, is to participate in a communal connection. This is why going to church, or clubs, or football games can be so important to so many people - in that community, where we are all connected with each other, when one person connects with Spirit we all experience the connection.

It doesn't matter what kind of community you're part of, so long as it's one that speaks to your heart and leaves you feeling open and joyful. Pay attention to the sensations and feelings you experience as part of the group. How does your body feel, moment to moment? How does your perception of life and of yourself shift as you spend time with the other people? What is it that you enjoy about being there and participating?

Again, noticing how these experiences contrast with your everyday life will tell you more about your relationship to the Sacred and how it expresses through you. And, when you are aware of the nature of these experiences, you can begin to recognise them for what they are – a taste of the experience of your own connection, unique and personal and changing.

Practice: Nature

"I can sing you a landscape
born of earth and stone and water
close enough to feel like home,
close enough to feel like home..."
Carolyn Hillyer, Riven Inside

Nature is what we call the non human world, from birds on telephone wires, to mud, to rain and rivers, to trees. The natural world is a wonderful place to connect to the Sacred; the spirits of plants, animals, and the elements are always aware of their connection to the greater whole, and can teach us a lot about being in harmonious relationship.

You may already have a favourite place to sit and contemplate, but don't worry if not - your back garden, local park or garden centre are all great places to experience nature. Anywhere that you can be with a plant, animal or natural elements like a river, earth or fire are all places that you can use to explore what nature holds for your relationship to the sacred.

Take some time to sit quietly and admire the beauty of nature. Allow all of your senses to participate; smell the rich dampness of earth, hear the music of trees in the wind and feel the warmth of a patch of sunlight on your skin. Allow your mind to fall away as you are immersed in your experience; recognise how you feel within yourself. Call for the great Spirit to be with you, and remember that the sacred lives within all things. Feel its presence around you, in the birds, the leaves and the wind.

Try out the different ways listed above to open up to the Sacred, as well as the suggestions in the next chapter and any other ways that come to you. You are looking for a personal experience of the Sacred, so pay attention to what feels best for you and be guided by your own knowing.

Don't worry if it takes some time for a sense of the Sacred to grow for you. Spirit is a powerful thing to witness, and if you have never experienced it before, or only experienced your connection briefly, you may find that your increase in awareness is naturally gradual. Enjoy the process and allow these new experiences to unfold at their own pace; like a flower opening when the conditions are right, our spiritual connection has its own schedule that we can't force, so we may as well relax and take our time.

Similarly, be open to however the experiences make you feel - there is no right or wrong way to connect with the Sacred, only your way. It's easy to assume that our connection with the Sacred will always take well-known spiritual expressions, but that simply isn't true. It's just as likely that your experience will be unlike anything you've ever heard of, or different to how you've ever thought about yourself or spirituality before. This is why it's so important to try things out for ourselves first, and to honour our uniqueness whenever we practice.

The Personal Sacred – Exploring Ways to Connect

...the beauty of shamanism is that a person's experience is neither right or wrong. Therefore, each person on a shamanic path learns to trust his or her own experience and not to follow any rules or doctrine.

Sandra Ingerman, Welcome Home

The next part of developing a sense of connection is to begin building a relationship with your personal sacred. To begin with, focus on exploring how it's best for you to work with your connection. Try lots of different simple practices and methods for creating a sense of sacredness or an awareness of spirit.

There are so many ways to connect with the Sacred - as many as there are people. No way is more or less right, and so long as it works for you, in the way that you need it, stick with it.

Likewise, any method or spiritual practice that doesn't feel right isn't likely to help you and may even hinder your ability to connect with Spirit. If you have an uncomfortable reaction to a practice or experience, take some time to explore why you had that reaction and to assess whether it was because it challenged an old assumption or belief that is no longer serving you, or whether it was because the practice wasn't right for you.

Below are some short descriptions of ways and methods to connect with the Sacred and to explore your relationship to it. The list is by no means exhaustive, and I'd encourage everyone to explore any and all other ideas that come to them, especially those ideas that bring excitement, passion or peace.

Practice: Shamanic Journeying

Shamanic journeying is an ancient spiritual practice that is used all over the world. It's called journeying because the practitioner travels to the Spirit World, meeting with their guides and other spirits to access healing and knowledge.

This may sound strange to us in our modern societies, but ancient peoples, as well as modern people that live in cultures which haven't forgotten this knowledge, know that there are two worlds - the physical world that we live in during the day, and the other, non-physical world that we can visit in our dreams and go to when we die. By journeying to this other world in a more conscious way, rather than in our sleep, we are able to work with Spirit more directly, to interact, learn and find solutions to our problems.

As a way of developing our connection with the Sacred, shamanic journeying is a powerful tool that allows us to speak with, see and experience directly the various aspects and faces of Spirit, and to bring back this knowledge into our daily lives so that it benefits us and our communities.

Journeying is usually taught in person during a workshop or when working with a shamanic practitioner, but it is possible to learn the basic method through a book. If journeying appeals to you and you would like to use it as a core practice in your relationship with the Sacred, I would recommend that you find an experienced teacher who can show you the various ways and maps of the Spirit Worlds that are needed to fully make use of this amazing tool.

To make your first shamanic journey, you will need to choose a time and place where you will not be disturbed, and have a drumming CD (or mp3) and your journal to hand. Many shamanic practitioners lie down to journey, and you may like to try this too, but you may find that you fall asleep quite easily at first! To stop yourself from falling asleep it can be useful to journey sitting up or to journey straight after your morning shower when you're refreshed and awake.

When you are ready to begin, open Sacred Space as you have practised, in the way that works best for you. As you do so, allow yourself to feel how the room around you changes as you become aware of Spirit all around you. Welcome and thank the Sacred for coming to you, and ask it to hold the space around you safely, guiding you on your journey for your highest good.

Before you start your journey, take some time to focus on why you're journeying. It can be helpful to write down or say out loud your specific intent - for example, "I'm journeying today to visit my personal space in the Spirit World for the first time" or "I'm journeying today to meet with my guide and ask how I can explore my relationship with Spirit".

For this first journey, it's important that your intent is to meet a guide for your journeying practice and to establish a relationship with them so that you can explore this new tool safely and effectively.

Once you have your intent held clearly in your mind, close your eyes and begin the drumming CD. Listen to the beat of the drum for a few moments, holding your intent clearly in your mind. Let yourself feel the sound as it passes through your body. Breathe gently and naturally, releasing any tension you've been holding and focusing on your intent to journey to the Spirit World.

As you listen, you may begin to feel different sensations; you body might feel as though it's drifting, or you might feel like you're shaking or moving even though you aren't. These sensations are different for everyone – simply let them come and go within you and keep your mind on your destination - the Spirit World.

You are going to a place that is just for you. It is a place that you've been to before, in your physical life, but now you're going in spirit. Allow the image of that place to form in your minds eye; see the ground beneath you, hear the sounds all around you, feel the warmth of the sun on your skin.

Take a deep breath and look around. Notice how this place is the same, but slightly different from the place you know in the physical world; it may have more plants growing in it, or it may be much brighter and more open, or it may simply have a glow about it that you've never seen before. Take all of this in.

Allow yourself to relax into this new awareness, and then bring your mind back to your intent for this journey – to meet a Journeying Guide who will help you learn about this practice. You may find that you want to call out loud for your guide to come to you, or you might find that a guide is already waiting for you when you arrive.

When you notice that someone is near you, allow yourself to focus on them so that their details become clearer to you. They may be a person, or an animal – be open to however they appear to you. Take in how they make you feel as well as how they look; do they feel right, do they feel good to be around? Do you feel like you recognise them in some way already? If so, speak to them and ask them if they're your guide, then listen for their answer – you may hear it, or simply know what they've communicated to you without any words.

If they don't feel right to you, turn away from them and keep calling for your guide to come to you until you see someone that you do feel comfortable with, or end the journey and come back at another time when you're more relaxed.

Once you've made contact with your guide, you can establish a relationship with them by asking what their name is and how they'd like to work with you, and by thanking them for their assistance. Take the time to become more familiar with their energy and how they appear to you, so that you can begin to recognise them more easily on every journey after this.

Stay for as long as you want, enjoying the beauty of your place and the company of your new guide, and when you want to return, simply call yourself back to your body. Allow the spirit world to slip away, and feel yourself pour back into the physical world; the sensations and sounds and colours of the room that you're in will come back, sometimes quickly and sometime gradually.

Take some deep breaths and wait for a few moments to let yourself adjust, then have a little stretch and look around to make sure that you're fully grounded back into your body. Note down in your journal anything that you noticed or any ideas you've had during your journey, and then close sacred space, thanking Spirit for its help and protection.

Once you're finished doing your journeying practice it's always a good idea to eat and drink something to help you ground back into your everyday life.

Practice: Working With Altars

Altars are symbolic spaces; when we create an altar we're really creating a place for us to step out of our everyday lives and experience our relationship with life and the Sacred in a more soulful way. An altar can be for general communion with Spirit, or it can be a place where you interact with a specific energy or archetype such as the land, your home, your marriage, or an angel or guide that you're working with.

To create an altar for your connection with the Sacred, you will need a collection of small objects that represent the Sacred and your relationship to it, such as candles, flowers, pebbles, seeds, gemstones, poetry, images and figurines, and an out of the way place where you can arrange the objects without them being disturbed. I've had great success with windowsills, radiator shelves and cabinets - you can even create your altar in your garden!

Once you've chosen your altar objects and the place for your altar, create a sacred space in the way that works for you, calling on the Sacred to be there with you. Ask for it to hold the altar and be with you when you come to work with it, paying attention to any sensations or ideas that come to you as Spirit enters the space.

Then, arrange the objects you have chosen in a way that feels meaningful to you. This is just the beginning of your altar, so don't worry about getting it 'right' – there is no right way, just your way! And the space will shift and change as you develop your connection, which is one of the powerful gifts of working with altars - they reflect your relationship back to you in a concrete, visible way so that you can work with it more consciously.

You could have a set amount of time during which you want to work with your altar, for example a week or a month, and a set time of day to be with your altar and enjoy its space. Alternatively, an altar can be somewhere that you go when you feel called, a more fluid part of your day rather than part of your routine. The important thing is that you spend time with your altar with the intent that you created it – in this case, to connect with the Sacred and become familiar with your relationship to it.

And while simply sitting with your altar and being aware of how you feel can be very powerful, it can also be helpful to bring offerings to the space, such as flowers, seeds, incense or things you have crafted, to nourish the work that you're doing. You can also move the objects around, add to them or take them away, as feels right to you, as well as doing other practices at your altar such as prayers and shamanic journeying, to see how being in this specifically created and personal space affects your experiences.

And when the time has come to dismantle your altar, whether it has been in place for days or months or even years, take the time to thank Spirit for being in the space for you and for working with you so directly. Take all the objects down and close the sacred space, and then give the whole area as well as your altar objects a good clean, either with incense, smoke, spirit water or breath. This is to make sure that no energy can linger, causing problems for you or your home.

Practice: Creating Ceremonies

Ceremony is another ancient spiritual practice that is used all over the world. It can have many forms and intents, from healing to worship to divination to celebration.

For our purposes here, let's define ceremony as a formal action witnessed by the Sacred. By this, I mean that it is something you do with a set purpose and format, and that you call on Spirit to be present when you do it.

An example would be planting a tree with the intent to give back to the earth. To make it a ceremony, you would say a prayer before and after the planting, telling Spirit why you were doing it, and you would include something symbolic, such as scattering offerings beneath the roots or tying a prayer flag to the trunk.

Ceremony is a wonderful way to connect with the Sacred, and can be as personal and meaningful as you want to make it. By stepping out of the ordinary rhythm of our lives and into the sacred space of ceremony, we create a safe place in our lives for us to be open to the Sacred.

Let your heart guide you as you create the ceremony - it knows what you need. And remember to recognise how you feel, how your body reacts to different ideas, and honour those feelings. Ceremony holds a lot of power, so make sure you respect it.

Be clear about what you are doing and why, and remember to call for the Sacred to be with you. Explore how different frameworks create a different experience for you, each expressing an aspect of your Sacred connection.

There are many ceremonies described throughout this book, all of which you can use to call for a greater sense of connection and a deeper understanding of your relationship with Spirit. From the Ceremonies for Change in section one to the ceremony for finding your BIG dream in the final section, try them all out and find out what works best for you.

One of the most powerful and beautiful things about ceremony is that it's always changing - that's what separates ceremony from ritual. Each time a ceremony is performed, it changes somehow, evolving as we evolve, reflecting our greater awareness. Ceremonies that were created centuries ago are still fresh now, because each person who performs them adds a little of themselves, personalises them and makes them relevant to how we live today.

It's this fluidity and openness to change that makes ceremonies so appropriate for working with our personal experience of the Sacred - it's just as powerful to create a ceremony that is totally unique to us, as it is to use a ceremony that is generations old.

Creating your own ceremony is very simple; you will need a specific intent - your reason for doing the ceremony in the first place - and a format or action that feels right for you. The action can be anything at all; you could light a fire, swim in a lake, eat a meal, pour a glass of wine into the sea, change your name, scatter flowers to the wind, walk over burning coals, sit in silent darkness, hike into the wilderness, say a prayer, make love, paint a picture, sing a song, or do any number of other things - so long as the action that you choose feels powerful and right to you, and your intent is strong and specific.

When you have decided on your action, and you have your intent clear in your mind or written down on paper, choose a place and time for your ceremony, remembering that the more time you give yourself to prepare, the more potent your ceremony will be. I recommend at least a day between deciding that you're going to hold a ceremony and performing the ceremony, but again, everything depends on intent and how it feels to you. Some of my most touching ceremonies have been done on the spur of the moment.

Everything leading up to your ceremony could be important and symbolic for you, from washing your hair to getting dressed to putting on music. When you're ready to begin, open sacred space and state your intent to Spirit; ask the Sacred to witness your ceremony and to hear your prayers, and then perform the action you've chosen with awareness and respect. Spend a little time absorbing the feelings and emotions your ceremony has given you before closing sacred space and returning to your day.

In the following weeks, you will find that changes and shifts happen in surprising ways. When we invoke the powers of Spirit and our own inner resources in this way, we access a power that has a much wider and deeper perspective on our lives than ourselves. This can mean that what we thought would happen, or what we thought we wanted, becomes revealed to us in a new, unexpected way, and even that things we assumed were impossible suddenly become very real indeed.

This is why it's important to respect the power of ceremony; be very clear and certain about the intent that you bring, and keep your ceremonies to aspects of your own life and connection rather than anyone else's.

Practice: Sandpaintings

A sand painting is a symbolic space, similar to an altar, that we create directly on the surface of the earth. They are fantastic tools for working with an issue or area of our lives that we'd like clarity on, because they show us visually how we're relating to the issue and what factors are involved for us, at a symbolic level.

To create a sand painting for your relationship with the Sacred, you will first need a small patch of earth. It can be grassy, on a beach, in a wood, or even in a pot on your windowsill! When you have this bit of earth to work with, open sacred space in the way that works best for you and call on the Sacred to hold your sand painting space while you work with it.

When you're happy with your sacred space and have taken a moment to focus on your connection to the Sacred and how you'd like the sand painting to help you explore it, look around for some objects that resonate with you. The objects you'll need can be anything - sticks or stones, pieces of paper or small plastic toys, really anything that comes to mind, is available in the area and feels right to you. The number of objects is also very open, so listen to you heart and let it guide you.

Once you have gathered your objects, sit with them in your sand painting space for a few moments. Hold them and touch them, letting yourself feel the various sensations and emotions, perceptions and ideas that make up your sacred connection. When you are ready, begin to arrange the objects within your sacred space, beginning with a border for your sand painting and then placing more objects within the centre to represent various aspects of your relationship with Spirit.

Let yourself be guided wholly by how you feel. Take only five minutes at the most to arrange your objects, so that you don't think too much about how to place them; remember, this is a symbolic space, something that the conscious mind cannot grasp fully.

Ask Spirit and the earth beneath your sand painting to work with your objects and your space over the next few days, showing you what you need to see and helping you to come into an even deeper, more open relationship with Spirit.

Leave the sacred space open over your sand painting for the next few days, and come back at least once a day to sit within your space. Allow yourself to be open to all the symbolic meaning of you sand painting, and notice any changes in the positioning of your objects. And don't be afraid to move the objects yourself to reflect how your understanding and feelings change over the days - a sand painting is a collaboration between you and the Sacred, not a static work of art.

Practice: Working With Medicine Objects
Medicine Objects are personal, symbolic objects that represent

specific aspects of our souls and our relationship with the Sacred. A medicine object can be anything, but they tend to be one of a number of traditional items such as drums, rattles, stones, feathers, sacred jewellery and carvings.

Many people have seen pictures of medicine objects in books or papers, but don't understand the meaning and powerful healing qualities of these important tools. A medicine object is like a bridge - through it we can directly and personally work with any aspect of ourselves, our environment, or Spirit to bring about greater knowledge and healing. Without medicine objects, our relationships with our spirit guides and spiritual practices can become ungrounded and stuck in a mental understanding, which means that we can't benefit from the full power of them.

Creating a medicine object is a distinctly personal process. Many people simply realise that they already have one, such as a special necklace that they've worn every day for years and represents their relationship with a particular saint or spiritual principle. Other people 'find' their medicine objects, feeling a call to work with an object without an understanding of why or how they made the connection. It's also possible to call for a medicine object - asking with our intent, often in ceremony, for an object to come to us to help us with a particular struggle or aspect we want to work with.

An example of this would be if we wanted to work with the aspect of ourselves that is comfortable and able to thrive within change. We could create a small ceremony to ask Spirit to send us an object to represent this aspect. The object could appear in our lives as a gift from a friend, an item in a shop that we recognise immediately, or something we find during the course of our day. We could dream about the object and then be required to make it, which often happens with medicine jewellery. Or we could be given the object as part of our work with a shaman or healer, such as when a shaman gifts a client with an object from their mesa, sharing their medicine.

To work with a medicine object is a personal practice that varies hugely between different people. Some people like to wear their object, perhaps on a cord beneath their shirt, or as a ring, and some even carry it around with them, such as shamans in my tradition who keep their mesa bundles with them every day. Other people like to keep their medicine objects on an altar or other special place, to work with when they're doing their spiritual practices.

Medicine objects can be helpful simply through the process of making or finding them, teaching us the lessons we need and helping us to see the aspect we're working with in a different light. They can also physically ground our work with spirit guides and spiritual teachers, for example when we decorate our medicine objects or blow what we have learned into them following an experience.

We can also ask our medicine objects questions by speaking with them, blowing our questions into them, meditating with them and journeying to meet them in the spirit world. Again, it's all about what feels right and works best for you.

Practice: Gratitude

"Waking up this morning, I see the blue sky.
I join my hands in thanks for the many wonders of life;
for having twenty-four brand-new hours before me."
Thich Nhat Hanh, Call Me By My True Names

Gratitude is a wonderful practice for finding and nourishing our spiritual connection that is practised by millions of people all over the world. Any time that we give thanks or appreciation for something in our lives, we are practising gratitude.

One way to include gratitude as a conscious spiritual practice for connecting with the sacred is to spend 5 minutes every day listing and giving thanks for every thing that you're enjoying in your life right now. You can list everything either in great detail, or very briefly; you can list hundreds of things or just your top ten; you can even practice this together as a family or community to increase the power of your appreciation and share the joy of the blessings in your life.

For example, during some of the most dark and difficult times in my life, practising gratitude has been the only spiritual practice that I had the energy or clarity to access. Being able to find even one thing to be thankful for, and spending just one minute focusing on that good thing in my life, has been the first step in recovering my connection with Spirit and accessing the healing I needed to recover and move forward in my life.

Gratitude is so powerful in this way because of our energetic natures. When we're feeling really low, our energy is vibrating at a low frequency. It can be very hard to use our Vision to see anything more positive, because of that low frequency in our energy fields. When we are able to see just one thing that is at a higher frequency than where we are, it opens us up to more of that higher frequency and creates a kind of snowball effect, bringing more of that higher frequency energy into us and weakening our attraction to the low frequency energy. This is why a gratitude practice is one of the first tools I recommend for people who are feeling depressed or stressed - it can literally open us up to all the other great tools and the power of our connection with the Sacred.

Practice: Music

Music is a beautiful and gentle way to open yourself to Spirit and experience the various tones of your connection. Begin with music that is emotional for you, that elicits a strong feeling in your body. Anything can work, and the music that works best will change depending on your well-being, mood and perspective at the time. The most important thing to remember is that this is your personal connection, so if temple chants or flute music doesn't feel right, that's OK - choose what works for you, rather than what you think is spiritual or sacred.

Practice: Poetry

Poetry is, at its best, a translation of the feelings and truths of the soul into words. Language is almost always a mental matter, expressing ideas, reason and limited perception, but in poems words can become doorways to the realm of spirit.

Any poetry can be soulful; my favourite poets for feeding my spiritual awareness are Thich Nhat Hahn and Rainer Maria Rilke. Choose poets whose words take your breath away, surrounding you in a bubble of stillness, and read them at a pace that's comfortable so that they can resonate fully.

Explore how different voices make you feel, and pay close attention to your inner senses as you read. There may be no need to call or invite spirit to you, as poems can do that themselves - just be open to the experience and welcome Spirit when you do notice its presence.

Reading poetry as a means to opening your connection to Spirit is something you can do anywhere - on the train, in the bath, even in the car if you have poetry on CD. No one else knows that you're communing with the divine. And if you memorise those poems that speak to you most strongly, you can take them with you everywhere.

Practice: Silence

Silence is an age old spiritual practice used in almost all traditions. In silence, we can no longer hide from ourselves; our minds must face their own patterns and habits, and we are isolated from a lot of what distracts us from the Sacred during everyday life.

To practice silence, you don't have to go to a mountain or a temple. The mundane noises of the world around us - the traffic, children across the street, the hum of electrical appliances - are part of the silence when you turn within. The most powerful way to find silence is to listen for it in your heart, at the centre of things.

Take the time to explore this practice, with the intent of connecting to the Sacred. Choose a place that is comfortable for you, and turn your attention within. There is no need to focus on anything in particular, to control your thoughts or to visualise anything. Simply be in the quiet and listen. You may find that thoughts come to mind, or that you get distracted, but that's fine. Just keep listening, noticing the silence that's beneath all of that. Invite Spirit to join you. Notice how you feel, and allow yourself to be open to the experience.

Many people would consider this to be a meditation practice, which I haven't specifically covered in this list of ways to connect – the subject is simply too large, and there are so many excellent books and teachers talking about it already. If you do find that practising with silence is helpful for you, you might like to seek out more information about the various meditation methods available and see if any work for you.

Practice: Movement

Movement can be anything from dancing to jogging to a martial art - it doesn't have to be yoga! When we move our bodies it's easier to get out of our heads and notice where we are. Try anything that makes you smile, feel alive or joyful. As you move, allow your thoughts to settle and turn your focus to your body - how does it feel? How does it want to move? Let your body tell you what it wants to do, and see how that makes you feel.

Once you're connected to your body, give yourself permission to feel the space around you. Let yourself feel from your centre, and then call for Spirit to be with you as you move. Notice the subtle sensations you get when Spirit is present, and how they change as your movement and mood change as well. Remember to go at your own pace and allow the experience to come naturally. And remember - if it doesn't feel right, don't do it!

Practice: Art

Artwork is another way that we translate the knowing of soul into something that can be consciously seen and felt. Like poetry, it is a powerful way of connecting to the sacred in a way that transcends our thoughts.

And you don't just have to enjoy other people's art! Try expressing your experiences of spirit on paper or in clay, allowing the feeling of connection to guide your hands. Remember to call to the divine as you work, and be open to whatever comes to you - it's not about creating something other people like, but about expressing and exploring your spiritual connection.

Practice: Community

Community is created when a group of people come together with a common intent. Just as groups can be destructive, they can also have great power for healing and sacred communion. Explore how you feel around different communities; each one will have an effect on your ability to connect and open to Spirit. Notice whether you laugh more or less, and how your heart feels. Be prepared to go outside of your comfort zone and try new things; your soul might be nourished by a cookery class or a climbing group. Just remember to pay attention to how you feel and your awareness of the Sacred as you explore.

There are so many ways to connect with the Sacred, more than I could ever list. That's the beauty of being unique souls - our experiences are all individual, and a whole world of opportunities is out there to be explored. So trust your own experience more than anything else - your heart knows who you are and where you are in your journey.

And remember to keep trying new things, no matter how long you've been walking your spiritual path; we are always changing, after all.

Growing a Relationship With The Sacred

Once we have an understanding of what the Sacred is to us and how we like to connect with it, we are able to develop a deeper relationship with it. It's important to do this because to be useful and effective for us in our daily lives, our connection with the Sacred has to have deep roots; we have to know how to work with it so that when we really need it, it can be there for us without us having to think about it too much. We have to learn how it feels for us, so that we can access it clearly and confidently when we're feeling a lot of other emotions and thinking lots of other thoughts.

Our relationship with the Sacred has to be something that is real and natural for us, otherwise it won't become part of our lives, which means it won't be able to make any real difference in our lives or in ourselves.

Like any other relationship in our lives, this relationship needs attention and time so that it grows and flourishes. And, like all relationships, it will have cycles and rhythms of its own; one of the most challenging things about walking a spiritual path is how our connection can change over time.

The practices and tools in the previous chapter were all about exploring our relationship with the Sacred. They work really well on their own, even if you only do them once. But to deepen our relationship, it can be helpful to connect on a regular basis and with some focus or purpose to guide us. This is because, while connecting occasionally and trying out different methods helps us to find the ways to connect that work for us, and to gain a first experience of the Sacred from various perspectives, to build a deeper relationship we must use those ways and methods that work for us to really experience all that the Sacred has to offer us.

Here are a few ideas for deepening your spiritual practice in your own way, using the experiences that you gained in the last chapter as a platform for further exploration and development. Remember to listen to your own heart and to change any instructions that don't work for you - this is about your relationship and your connection, not anyone else's, so it has to work for you!

Practice: Creating a Daily Routine

Creating a daily routine is a common way to maintain your spiritual practice over time. But while it can be tempting to think something up and implement it immediately, a more measured approach can be more effective.

From your exploration of the different ways to connect with the Sacred, you will know which practices and tools work best for you. Pick one of these core practices and try to do it every day for a week. Plan the time into your daily routine and make an effort to do the practice no matter what. (This is also an act of power, which we will be exploring and using in the section on courage.)

Your daily practice need not be long or complicated. Ten minutes a day of heartfelt prayer or exuberant, mindful dancing is a powerful and nourishing spiritual habit that will permeate the rest of your day.

Practice: Creating a Structure

Creating a structure is another powerful way to focus the development of your spiritual path. By setting down a framework for your practice, you'll be able to consciously choose how you grow and develop.

Through your exploration of your connection to the Sacred, you may have questions about yourself, Spirit, or your path. Or you may have come across a practice or area of your spirituality that particularly peaks your interest. These questions and interests are perfect for deeper work; focus on exploring them during your daily practice.

For example, if you had discovered during periods of

meditation that you are very physically tense, you could set down a period of a month to work with that tension through your daily shamanic journeying. You could ask your guides for a practice specifically for transforming tension, you could journey to find the root of your anxiety and you could work on looking for the gift of tension in your life.

Another example would be if you felt drawn to ceremony. You could spend each week working with one traditional form of ceremony, keeping this structure for four weeks, six weeks, or even longer.

The point of creating and following a structure in this way is to focus your intent on a particular area of personal growth.

Practice: Meeting and Working with Guides

Working with guides and other spiritual beings or archetypes is another way of developing our relationship with the Sacred. The divine exists in and as all things - when we work with spiritual guides we are working with an aspect of the greater whole. This allows us to strengthen challenging relationships and to become intimate with the faces of Spirit that truly speak to us.

A spirit guide or ally can communicate with us when we meditate, visualise, pray, sit in silence, create poetry or art, journey or when we are asleep.

When we work with other spirits, it's important to remember our boundaries - just as we do when we work with other humans. Never do or allow anything that doesn't feel right in your heart - learn to listen to your inner knowing and respect it.

You have already met a spirit guide through the journeying practice in the first section, and you may know others from previous experiences and practices. If you feel that you need it, you can also call for another guide to come and work with you for more specific practices and healing.

To meet a new spirit guide that you can work with on your spiritual path, it's best to do a shamanic journey to the spirit world. Create sacred space and set your intent for your journey as usual, asking for a spirit guide to meet you on the journey who can help with the specific area you want to work with.

When you reach the spirit world, connect to your usual journeying guide and then call for your new guide to join you and watch for them to arrive. They could be in any shape; it's common for guides to take the form of an animal or mythological figure. But don't worry if your guide looks like a normal person either!

Introduce yourself to the guide and thank them for coming. It's polite to offer them a gift - you will find that one appears nearby or in your hands for you to give them.

Ask what they'd like to be called and how they would like to be worked with. They may have a particular place they'd like to meet, or a special thing they'd like you to do in their honour. Many like to be fed with an offering of incense or spirit water.

When you return from your journey, write down what you've experienced in your journal. And remember to honour any agreements that you made with your new guide so that the relationship gets off to a good start.

Once you have a spirit guide for a certain area of your life and you know how to work with them, you can take any questions or problems to them. This is a great way to become really familiar with an aspect of the Sacred, as well as a good foundation for any personal healing work you do. What you do need to remember, though, is that these beings are guides and teachers, and their help is in the form of healing and support rather than telling you what to do or solving your problems for you.

Developing Trust

Trust is the ability to be open, to feel comfortable and safe in a relationship. For any relationship to be healing, loving and empowering, there must be trust. When we trust the Sacred, we have something in our lives that cannot be lost or stolen or destroyed. When we know from experience that spirit comes when we call, and how we can work with it, then we have a still, safe place to be no matter what else is going on around us.

To develop trust, we have to show trust; we have to give the Sacred and our spiritual path the chance to prove to us that we can rely on them - we have to go to them when we need help. This can be anything from looking for a moment of peace during a stressful day, to looking for healing during an illness, to asking for help when we need to make a tough decision. Every time that we give the Sacred an opportunity to love us, and the Sacred comes to be with us, our trust grows.

It's important here to note here that trust isn't about Spirit always doing what we ask, or our spiritual path always making things easy and comfortable for us. We will still face challenges and struggles - the important thing is that our relationship with the Sacred is always there for us when we need it, and that it continues to serve our peace and well being in the way that is truly best for us.

Trust is a very personal thing that is unique to each of us; what creates trust in one person could leave another cold. Think about a time when you felt your trust was earned, or rewarded - what was it about that situation that made you feel safe, valuable and comfortable enough to be more open about yourself, or to show vulnerability?

For some people it can be physical acts that engender trust, like being take care of when they are ill or being supported in achieving a physical goal. For others, trust is based more on emotional support, like being given the time and space to express our feelings, or having our preferences and emotional needs met by someone close to us.

Whatever it is that makes you feel more able to rely on someone or something, to trust them with more of who you are and what you really need, that's what you need to find within your relationship with the Sacred.

The exercises and practices below can help you to find those keys to your trust, and to actively work with them in your spiritual connection so that Spirit becomes a strong and reliable ally for you in your everyday life.

Practice: Gratitude – A Practice In Trust

Gratitude is more than just a practice, it can be a spiritual path in and of itself. And one of the wonderful ways that gratitude can be really helpful for us is as a practice for developing our trust in the Sacred.

To work with gratitude in this way, we take account of all of the blessings we have been given in our lives and work to realize that all of those things could have happened very differently.

Take some time to sit with your journal somewhere quiet and peaceful. List five of the best things that have even happened in your life - they don't have to be big things, just things that you're really grateful to have experienced, like sitting on the beach and watching the sun come up, giving your child a kiss goodnight, the first night you met your partner, or achieving a qualification.

Sit with how great those things make you feel, and allow yourself to see how they have impacted other areas of your life. And now see how easily those experiences could have happened differently, or not at all.

This isn't about making ourselves feel bad or worried, so don't think too hard or imagine what it would have been like if those things hadn't happened. Rather, just notice the small coincidences and chances that, when added together, turn your beautiful experience from a mundane, normal occurrence into a miracle. For example, the bus could have been 3 minutes late and you'd have had to rush your meeting with your partner after you came home from work, rather than taking the time to really express how glad you were to see each other. Or the sky could have been cloudy, meaning that your time on the beach was cold and dark rather than touchingly beautiful.

It's easy to see, when you look at the most precious experiences of your life, that in a very everyday way you have been taken care of and given a blessing that otherwise would not have happened. At first, these blessings can seem like chance, or coincidence. But when you begin to see them all together, the pattern emerges; there are times for all of us when the grace of the Sacred steps in and directs our path, when we let it. It has been doing this all of our lives, providing everything needed for our survival which could so easily have been missing, from the plants that are grown by the earth and rain and sun over weeks and months, to the immense organisation that goes into building our houses, to the very cells of our body, all miraculously functioning without our conscious control.

When we can look at life in this way, we see how supported we have been, and can begin to learn the patterns of give and take that the Sacred works with in this physical world, ultimately learning to trust them and how they will work in our lives.

Practice: Asking for help

Another powerful way that we can develop trust in the Sacred is to ask for its help. Once we have a solid foundation of practices and tools that we can use to access our spiritual connection, we can begin to work with that connection in the everyday occurrences of our lives. While some people find this a strange idea, or even an inappropriate one, asking for help and grounding our relationship with the Sacred into our daily lives is the basis of practical spirituality.

When we ask for help, and allow the Sacred to provide that help in its own way, we begin to learn even more about how our relationship with the Sacred really works, and how it fits into our lives. Doing this turns our spirituality into something practical, grounded and even more beautiful.

And when we ask for help, and Spirit provides that help, we learn that our spiritual connection is something that is truly, practically there for us - we learn to trust it in a meaningful way.

Through your experiences in the previous chapters, you'll already have some good ideas about how to ask for help from the Sacred. Many of the connection practices enable us to have a dialogue with Spirit, and to receive guidance in return, and some even allow us to work energetically with the Sacred to bring about changes within ourselves and our lives.

As a beginning practice, I'd particularly recommend working with sandpaintings as a means of asking for spiritual help and guidance in your life. This is such a great trust-building tool because it allows us to see things from a different perspective, one that is visual and physical rather than mental - this means that we can be more open to the guidance of Spirit, which is often symbolic or subtle.

Journeying and ceremony are also great trust-building practices, allowing us to interact personally with the Sacred, ask questions and build up experiences of calling for Spirit to be with us, and having that call answered.

But ultimately, use whatever practices work best for you. Simply asking for help or support, either out loud or silently, is enough to call the wisdom and healing of the Sacred into your life. As with all of these practices and tools, it's the intent that you have at the time that really matters.

Asking the Sacred for help can take many forms and have many outcomes, from asking for energetic healing to guidance on choosing a home, from keeping us safe as we travel to bringing about deeper understanding and connection with our partners.

The most important thing to remember is that when we ask for help we have to be open to receiving it, in the way that it is given. Clinging to a particular outcome or solution, and getting frustrated or downhearted because Spirit isn't giving it to us is a sure way to lose trust rather than gain it. This is why having a solid relationship with the Sacred is important before we begin to really work with it actively in our lives - if we don't understand how Spirit works in our lives, it can be easy to make assumptions about how and when and why the Sacred intervenes for us, leading to confusion. It takes time to learn how to accept and be open to the Sacred without clinging, without holding on too tightly and shutting out the magical support that can come to us when we let go of our pre-conceived ideas about how things 'should' go.

The Open Heart

"Love is the only freedom that exists in the world..."
Khalil Gibran

There comes a time in our relationship with Spirit when we become able to open up; trust has been created and is growing within us, we are familiar with the Sacred and how it works in our life, and we know how connection feels to us.

This is the point which mystics and seekers have described for centuries - the moment when we fall in love with God. This may sound strange, or even a bit unnerving, to you, but it's not. You have been building a relationship with Spirit, and just like any other relationship in your life it's natural at a certain point to feel love.

And it is this point, more than any of the other practices and experiences we have explored, that provides us with a new way to perceive change. Through our explorations of our spiritual connection we may now have different and helpful maps to navigate various transformations, from death to career changes to economic downturns. These maps are empowering ways in which to re-orientate ourselves so that we are more comfortable with the way everything is moving around us.

But when we open our hearts to Spirit, from a place of trust and personal experience, we are able to access something more. In those moments that we are able to do this, and in the memories of these moments, we find infinity - we experience the place where we are Spirit, and Spirit is us. We experience a taste of what is forever unchanging.

Until you have experienced your particular flavour of this, it's hard to imagine. It is a moment of enlightenment - bringing light to what is, so that we can truly see our lives and ourselves. In the face of that light, no transitory physical or mental change is truly unsettling.

What I can tell you is that you will know it when you experience it, and that it isn't a single event but rather a continuum - a state of being that grows within you, becoming a stronger and stronger source of empowerment and well-being that affects every aspect of your life.

Opening to the Sacred isn't something that will happen overnight, or when you consciously decide to do it. Like so many transformations, it is a process rather than an event, and it usually happens over a long period of time, often without you even noticing it.

This is because it's not a function of our minds - something that we can mentally understand in a way that accurately reflects the reality of our experience. Rather, it's an experience of our hearts and souls, our unconscious awareness, and even our bodies.

Saying this, there are some things that we can do to prepare for and encourage this process of opening and complete connection. The first and most important thing, when we feel we are ready, is to give ourselves permission and to state our intent to be more open and present with the Sacred. As we've already explored, intent is more powerful than any action on its own, and when we combine a strong intent with a ceremony to express that intent, we are communicating in the language of spirit and soul. By doing this, by calling for the Sacred to guide us, support us and facilitate us in opening our hearts to our spiritual connection, we are creating a powerful momentum that will carry us in that direction.

Below is a simple ceremony that you can use to begin the journey of opening your heart to the Sacred. As always, if this ceremony feels right to you then please do use it, but if not, have the confidence to respect your own inner guidance and let your heart tell you what you need to do. And remember as well that there is no race or rush, and that developing our connection with the Sacred is something we can only do in our own time, when we are truly ready.

Practice: The Open Heart Ceremony

One of the most beautiful ceremonies that I know is the Despacho ceremony, which comes from the Andes in South America. A Despacho is at its most simple an offering ceremony, where various symbolic items are offered in gratitude and prayer. In the Andean tradition, there are over a hundred different forms of Despacho ceremony, each for a specific intent and purpose, and each with specific ingredients.

While many of the ingredients of a traditional Despacho ceremony aren't available outside of the Andes, we can still use this powerful ceremony to carry our prayers and to re-create harmony in our lives.

The Open Heart Ceremony is a Despacho ceremony, that uses the fundamental, traditional form to express our prayers for open hearted connection with the Sacred. Like any other ceremony or practice in this book, follow your feelings about this ceremony and change any ingredients or instructions if you feel that's needed. The most important aspect is, of course, your intent and your connection with the Sacred.

To do an Open Heart Despacho ceremony, you will need:

- a piece of paper
- some thread
- some offerings to give, such as sweeties, chocolate, sugar, seeds, raisins, oats, flower petals, a thimble of wine, or anything else that may symbolise what you are offering thanks for
- three bay leaves or leaves from a plant that you feel connected to, picked with respect

Collect all of the items you will need in a quiet place where you will not be disturbed. You might like to play some gentle music, to light a candle, or to meditate for a while before beginning. Take some deep breaths and allow yourself to become centred and still, and then begin the ceremony.

Create a sacred space around you by calling out to the four directions of North, South, East and West, and then the Earth and Sky, asking them to hold you as you make your offering. Then, call to Spirit, asking for it to be with you and to guide you in your ceremony. You can also call on any guides, ancestors or teachers that you work with to be present and part of the ceremony as well.

Once you have created the sacred space, place the piece of paper in front of you and fold it into thirds both horizontally and vertically so that it has six squares marked on it. Lay the paper out in front of you, so that the folded sides form a bowl around the centre square, which is where you will place your offerings.

Sit for a few moments, letting yourself remember what you are praying for. Let the sense of your connection with the Sacred fill you as you call to mind each beautiful and supportive experience you have had as part of your spiritual journey, and each way that your life has been changed or touched by these experiences.

When you are ready, pick up one of the offerings you prepared, and blow one of these experiences into it, filling it with your grateful intent to open to an even deeper experience of Spirit. Then put the offering into the central square of the paper, where ever you feel called to place it.

Continue to blow your experiences and connection into the offerings, placing them into your bundle where and how feels right to you.

When you are ready to complete the ceremony, take the three leaves and hold them while you focus again on the deep connection you have with the Sacred. Into the first leaf, blow all of your appreciation for the blessings and experiences that this relationship has given you. Then, place the leaf into the bundle, letting go of that old phase of your relationship as you do so.

Into the second leaf, blow all of your dreams for the new phase of your spiritual connection. Give gratitude for the opportunities and gifts this phase will bring you, and then release it to Spirit as you place the leaf into the bundle beside the first.

Into the last leaf, blow your sense of the Sacred and your connection to it, which is always there and will always be there for you to rely on and enjoy. Place the final leaf into the bundle and take a moment to absorb the beauty of your offering.

When you are finished admiring how beautiful your relationship with the Sacred is, fold the rest of the paper over the bundle, being careful to keep all of the offerings inside. Tie the bundle with some thread, red and white is good as it represents the sacred masculine and feminine combined. Then place your bundle somewhere safe and quiet until you are ready to complete the ceremony out in nature.

Finally, close the sacred space by thanking each direction for holding your ceremony, and by thanking your ancestors, guides, teachers and Spirit for witnessing your offering and hearing your prayers.

To complete the ceremony, you will release the bundle to Spirit, either by placing it in a fire, giving it to running water or the sea, or by burying it in the earth. Create a sacred space, just like when you made your bundle, and let go of your Despacho as you give it to the elements and to Spirit for them to transform. Traditionally, we turn our backs on the offering once it has been made, symbolically letting go of any expectations and attachments to the outcome of the ceremony. When you are ready, close the sacred space like you did before.

A heart that is open to the Sacred is not something that can be rushed, or even consciously created. It is a process, one that comes through developing our spiritual connection, learning to trust and letting our souls lead us.

And it is not a switch that is either on or off, either; enlightenment is a process of ever opening and deepening connection, rather than an attainment or goal. When we live in tune with our hearts and continue to grow, those moments of light will come. And they will also go, so try not to focus on them but to enjoy them, creating spaces for them in your life.

Section Three:

Truth

...acquired knowledge is merely hearsay in the presence of
divine insight...
Rumi

Truth is usually defined as 'that which is in accordance with fact or reality', and while many people take this to mean scientific fact exclusively, shamans, mystics and spiritual seekers know that the truth is actually a much broader set of understandings and knowledge. The word 'true' originally meant faithful or trustworthy - that which we can rely on. When we understand truth in this sense, we can see how important it is for living with change, and how it is actually a much more personal standard than simply 'that which our society commonly considers to be fact'.

Truth is actually what we can personally rely on as a trustworthy understanding or map of our reality; for it to be useful and meaningful, it can only come from personal experience, from within, because if it has no personal foundation and is only based on what we've been told by others, we can't rely on it - we can't know that it's really the truth for our own lives rather than a truth that only works for someone else.

What this means is that our truth is something we are always growing and learning about, and grounding into our lives. It is based on what we have experienced up until that point, that which we know and can trust.

Truth is important in our lives because without it, we have no solid ground to stand on as we interpret the world around us. If we don't know what we can rely on, what is trustworthy in our lives, then when everything is changing we can easily become lost and confused, making assumptions about what is happening and forgetting what is really important to us.

Do you remember what it's like to spin and spin around, something that all children play at? The world blurs and whirls around you, and if you don't keep your eyes on something still it's all too easy to loose your balance and fall over. That's what our truth is - that still point we can rely on to always be there for us, helping us to make sense of the whirling, blurring world as it changes around us. When we can access that 'still point of the turning world', change can be transformed from something frightening and uncomfortable into something thrilling and exciting.

Developing a sense of personal truth comes from experience and practice. Have you ever met an elderly person who had a sense of peace around them, within whom you recognised wisdom and a grace beyond simple age? That person has developed their own truth, simply through bringing awareness to their many life experiences; they have found a still place within themselves that they can rely on in their outer life.

We can all do the same, because we all have experiences, everyday, that we can learn from and find our own truths within. And when we focus on developing that sense of truth, we begin to grow an ability to discern for ourselves, an instinct for what rings true and what doesn't.

This is something that has to be developed and honed - if we begin to pick and choose what's true without grounding our instincts in experience, we can fool ourselves and eventually get lost. What is important is to build up a body of personal experience of looking for the truth, learning what it feels like and how it works in your life, so that when you're in a situation where you need to apply the solid foundation of your truth you already have confidence that your knowing is trustworthy.

Other People's Truths

"So the wise soul watches with the inner not the outward eye,
letting that go,
keeping this."
Lao Tzu, Tao Te Ching

Part of practising and growing the power of truth, in conjunction with connection, courage and vision, is practising mindfulness when it comes to the truths and perceptions we are offered by other people. It's very easy, especially in areas of life that we don't feel like experts about, to give up the power and responsibility of truth to someone else. Often, we begin to do this when we're very young, avoiding being honest about what our own experiences and perceptions have taught us and adopting other, less authentic, viewpoints instead.

We do this for so many reasons - to avoid insulting someone we care about, to avoid confrontation, or to please someone we know cares about us. Sometimes we do it because we're under-confident about our own authority, like when we allow doctors or other experts to explain away our very real and important experiences because they 'know more than we do'. And sometimes we do it because the thought of taking the action or committing to the knowledge that we know is true and right for us just seems like too much work, trouble or 'being difficult' when it would be easier to go along with the crowd.

The problem with giving up our own truths for the truths of others is that we lose access to the inner power that comes with that truth. Our truth is our authentic and unique way of seeing and experiencing life - if we throw it away, we are throwing away all that individual expression, as well as all the unique insights and opportunities that only we can see. When we reject our truth, what we are really doing is rejecting our own authority, connection, vision and voice - essentially, all the aspects of ourselves that make us powerful, and help us to thrive within our lives, and within change.

Adopting someone else's truth, especially when it feels wrong to us, is a kind of betrayal. It is a betrayal of our souls and of the unique life that Spirit has given to us, and only us. Another person's truth will never be grounded in our personal experiences, and no matter how adamant that other person is, they can never know your experiences and so they can never know what your personal truth really is.

Obviously, we live in a world that's full of facts and opinions - it comes from the internet, books, films, and all the hundreds and thousands of people who we interact with and who influence our perceptions of the world. And we need to use most of this information to get along in modern life, at least to a degree that doesn't leave us paralysed with confusion or indecision.

A huge amount of the information you come across won't make you feel either one way or the other - it will neither resonate strongly with you, nor make you feel oddly wrong and uneasy. This isn't truth, or knowledge - it's simply information; a collection of understandings and mental constructs that tell us how to navigate in this world, and are fine for us to use. We just need to remember that they aren't necessarily true, just useful in that moment.

When we can use information in the way that serves us, remaining unattached to it, we can still choose to access our own truths when the need arises. The problem comes when we start to ignore the truth of our own experience in favour of this informational map, or for the truths that other people want us to adopt.

By the time we come to begin practising truth, as part of becoming comfortable with change, we may already have absorbed and adopted some truths that originally came from other people. The process of letting go of other people's truths has to start way back, deep in our unconscious and our past, and the way to do this is to use ceremony.

Practice: Letting Go Of Other People's Truths

Many of us have developed a habit of accepting information from outside sources and becoming reliant on it, instituting it as 'the truth' within our understanding of the way the world works. Most of this information was never supposed to be used like this, and once it outlives it's usefulness it actually begins to get in the way of our well-being.

Unfortunately, these beliefs have become so ingrained, and so unconscious, that we are often totally unaware of their effects on us - we go about our days, programmed with information that is inappropriate for our own lives and the experiences we are having, and don't understand what's holding us back.

The unconscious nature of these old beliefs means that working at the level of myth and ceremony is going to be the most powerful method of moving forward. Ceremony allows us to access our deepest selves, calling on the forces of the Sacred and our own souls to create transformation that goes beyond the conscious and affects every area of our lives. A ceremony can initiate a great change within us faster than any mental or psychological tool.

To perform this ceremony, you will need:

- somewhere safe to hold a fire, either out of doors or inside, in a fire proof bowl
- some kindling and some small pieces of wood
- matches or a lighter
- a burnable offering such as a stick or some flowers
- a piece of paper and a pen

Choose a time when you can be alone and undisturbed, and sit in silence with your piece of paper and pen for a few moments. Allow the busy thoughts of the day to fall away, and take a few deep breaths, letting your body relax as you do so.

Your may like to open sacred space and ask for guidance, or to listen to some beautiful music, or to ask for your guides to be with you. Once you feel centred and ready, begin to call up into your awareness any beliefs you've been holding that no longer feel authentic.

Let them come into your mind. Just watch them, rather than think about them, and notice the basic belief that each one contains. You may find that many come to mind, or only one or two, or even none at first. That's ok, just be aware and open for these old beliefs to surface.

For example, you may have a belief that 'money does not grow on trees' – meaning that it's hard to come by, or that the meaning of love is sacrifice, or that we shouldn't look at the past and allow ourselves to feel it's effects - 'there's no use crying over spilt milk'.

Once you have an idea of what each of them is, jot them down on the piece of paper, quickly and without thinking. You don't have to write very much, or even write in sentences - you just need a note for each of them. You can even add a little note for 'any other's I haven't remembered', just to make sure you've got them all!

Put the paper to one side and keep it safe while you prepare for your ceremony, closing sacred space if you opened it and thanking Spirit and your guides for their support.

That evening, take your piece of paper and other ceremonial supplies to the place you have chosen for your ceremony. Pause for a moment to take in the space around you; feel the earth beneath you and the sky above you, feel the breeze, or notice any distant sounds. Allow your breath to come naturally and let go of any thoughts or ideas about how the ceremony should go.

Simply be in the moment and relax.

When you are ready, open sacred space in the way that works best for you, calling for the Sacred to be with you and to witness your ceremony. Call for any guides or spirit teachers to be with you as well, and take a moment to enjoy their supportive presence and to tell them how happy you are to be with them again.

Then build your fire, either in your fire pit or in your fire proof bowl. Lay out some kindling first, and then lay the bigger pieces of wood on the top, stacking them so that they are positioned evenly apart and are the right size for the space you're working in. When you're happy with your fire, use your lighter or matches to light the kindling.

Take a few moments to call for the fire to join you as the flames catch. Welcome the spirit of fire to your ceremony and tell it, either out loud or silently, your intent to let go of old, unhelpful beliefs. Watch the flames build for a while; you could sing or dance, or rattle, or just sit in silence, whatever feels right to you.

When the fire is burning well and you feel that it's time to perform the ceremony, take your piece of paper and hold it up in front of you. Blow on it, letting all of those old beliefs and ideas that no longer serve your well-being flow from your breath into the paper. Keep blowing until you feel that all the beliefs have been released, then place the paper on the fire. Let go of the beliefs as you do so, and ask the fire to take them and transform them for you as it burns the paper.

Take some time to let yourself feel the transformation, breathing deeply and clearly holding your intent to accept these changes.

Once the all of the paper has burnt away, pick up your offering and hold it up in front of you like you did with the paper. Blow into it all of your gratitude and thanks for the fire and for Spirit, for their help and support of you as you make this change, and then respectfully place that in the fire as well.

Spend some time beside the fire as it burns down. This is a good time to reflect on your ceremony and to envision how you're going to move forward now that you've made this big change. Trust that the transformation you have initiated through the ceremony will now begin to shift various situations in your life, reflecting the shifts within you. And know that the transformation will be at your own pace, in the way that is best for you.

When you are finished and the fire has burnt down to embers, thank Spirit and the fire for hearing your call and close sacred space.

Practice: Finding My Truth - A Practice In Mindfulness

While washing the dishes one should only be washing the dishes, which means that while washing the dishes one should be completely aware of the fact that one is washing the dishes.
Thich Nhat Hanh, Miracle of Mindfulness

Once we have begun the process of letting go of old, unhelpful truths we can begin to work on our discernment when it comes to adopting new truths.

Have you ever been in a conversation and agreed to something that you later felt very uneasy about? Or have you ever heard someone make an assertion, maybe on the news or on a TV show, that gave you an uncomfortable feeling in your stomach? If you have, you may have just experienced a belief that comes from someone else, but that you have adopted without really finding out if it's actually true for you personally.

It's a very easy thing to do; there are many people who would like us to accept their point of view over our own, for various reasons. We each have our own motives for doing obliging them, from people pleasing to a fear of the actual truth, to not wanting to make a fool of ourselves. But that uneasy feeling isn't there for nothing - it's telling us that what we're doing, the information we're accepting and adopting as truth, just doesn't sit right with us and may actually be unhelpful to us.

A very simple and effective practice that we can all use to manage the truths that we adopt as our own is mindfulness. Mindfulness is most associated with Buddhist meditation, but it can be found in various forms in almost all spiritual traditions. It is a state of open acceptance and awareness of the moment, and all that we are experiencing within it.

When we're in a mindful state, we are aware of the various ideas and sensations that we're experiencing as we experience them. This means that when we think, "Oh, that doesn't feel right," or we get a sensation of discomfort and unease, we are more likely to notice and then be able to act on it. So we are less likely to unintentionally accept and adopt someone else's truth rather than listen to our own experience and perception.

To practice mindfulness is both very simple and surprisingly challenging. Maintaining a high level of inner awareness in every moment is something that many of us haven't learnt how to do yet, but it is just a matter of practice - which is why it's called a practice!

To begin with, try to dedicate 5 minutes of each day for one week, at whatever time works for you, to your mindfulness practice. You don't have to sit in a room on your own to do your practice, because you can bring your awareness to anything you do in your life, from washing the dishes to driving the kids to school to having a conversation. But if you do feel it would be easier to begin in a quiet and still place, then by all means do that.

Remember that mindfulness is about open acceptance of whatever you are experiencing. Rather than focusing on a particular thought or state of emotion you are simply being with what is - letting yourself notice all the tiny impulses, ideas, feelings, sensations and distractions. Allow your mind to notice and acknowledge each of these as they arise within you, and then let them go and return to the constant sensation of your breathing, which is always there to remind you of the present.

As you do this, you will begin to notice patterns in your thinking. Emotions may come up inside you, or you may become distracted by a particular train of thought. Don't let this worry you, but just return your attention to the present moment as soon as you notice that you've wandered.

Do this practice every day for one week, and see what happens. See how it feels to bring mindfulness to your everyday activities, becoming more aware of your inner state and how it's responding to the world around you. If you really like working with mindfulness, you could even make it your core daily practice.

Once you have developed a bit more awareness of yourself in the moment, you will then be able to bring that awareness to how you adopt ideas and information from other people. Notice how you feel about certain statements of belief, and honour those feelings as you go about your day.

Once you have recognised a situation where you are being offered a belief to adopt and turn into your truth, ask yourself some questions. Does this belief fit with what you've learnt through previous experiences? How does it feel to you, deep down inside - does it sit well, or does it feel incomplete, or uncomfortable?

Sometimes what's true isn't always easy for us to accept, and can be frightening or painful for the parts of us that are attached to an old way of seeing things. But your heart will be able to recognise the truth when it sees it, so listen to it and know that you don't have to completely commit to a particular interpretation of reality to be able to make use of it, and especially not in order to please anyone else.

The Heart of Spirit

One of the places that we find our most potent personal truth is at the heart of our relationship with Spirit. This is the source of all our spiritual experiences, our personal connection with the Sacred - which is another reason why developing an ability to experience our connection with the Sacred is so important for becoming comfortable with change.

It is in this place, where we directly experience the essential nature of life and ourselves in relation to life, that we can learn some of the most valuable truths - what is the Sacred for us, how does the Sacred work and act in our lives, how do we relate to the Sacred, what can we trust about the Sacred, and how do we ourselvesquiet fit into the rest of creation? These are all hugely important questions that no one else can answer for us - only we can, through experiencing the answers ourselves as part of our connection with Spirit.

Finding the truth that comes from our spiritual connection involves being aware, being mindful. It's so easy when we're exploring our spirituality to become overwhelmed by the newness of it, or to look for specific feelings and experiences that we think we should be having. When we compare our experiences to other people's standards in this way, or push our development too quickly, we lose sight of what we're actually experiencing, in that moment. And then we miss the real benefits and gifts of our connection with the Sacred.

It's very common, even for people with lots of experience of spiritual practices, to assume that we need to feel a certain type of sensation or emotion as part of our connection - that we're not doing it right if we're not seeing pretty lights, or feeling waves of energy, or transforming our perception of the world in a dramatic way. But spiritual experiences are unique to the person and the moment, and they are often very subtle, bringing transformation to our lives in a quiet, unassuming way; our pre-conceptions about spirituality can get in the way of these real experiences.

The practices in this section all focus on creating awareness of our own experiences, so that we can find the truth of them for ourselves. And the first practices I recommend beginning with, especially if you've been working with your connection for a little while, are all about finding the heart of Spirit - the truth that lives within your relationship with the Sacred.

Practice: Finding Patterns in Our Experiences of the Sacred

Take some time out of your routine to sit quietly with your journal. You might like to connect with Spirit in your favourite way before you begin the practice, or you may simply want to sit for a few moments to relax and let your everyday thoughts and feelings subside.

When you are feeling ready, allow all of the experiences you have had with the Sacred come to mind. Remember them as they come, letting yourself connect with all the feelings and insights you experienced at that time. Don't try to make any sense of them or to think about them for the moment, just let the memories become more present within you.

Begin to jot down these memories of your connection with the Sacred, using a few words or sentences. Keep it short, don't let yourself think too much about it, just let yourself feel the experiences and then note down something that will anchor that feeling for you. Don't worry about writing neatly, or in the lines, or even from right to left - just let the words flow as they come and put them down on the pages wherever they feel right.

Let all of the experiences come and be noted, and when you stop having new memories come up just put down your pen.

You may have three or four memories jotted down, or ten, or even more. The most important thing at this point is that you've expressed a little of those feelings onto the paper, in a way that feel clear and authentic to you.

Put your journal aside and leave it for a little while, maybe even a day or two. When you come back to it later, take some more time to sit and settle within yourself before opening it to the pages where you noted down your memories. Read over your notes, quickly at first, and then read them again - this time focus on noticing any words that are repeated, or written larger, or with more strength in the handwriting. Notice which words seem to jump out when you just glance at the paper. Notice which words generate a feeling within you when you read them or say them aloud.

These words are important - they are signposts to the truths of your connection with the Sacred. Read them over; you might like to write them down on a separate page and decorate them, or put them up on your wall or on an altar if you are working with one.

Another way to find the patterns in your experiences of the Sacred is to work through your spiritual explorations to find common themes - feelings or ideas that have come up repeatedly, or been particularly important and effective in your life.

Make a list in your journal of all the ways to connect that you have explored personally. Beside each of these methods write some notes about your experiences, how they felt, and how they have impacted on you and your understanding of the world.

What sensations, emotions and perceptions have you often experienced? Which feelings do you experience every time you connect with the sacred? And which feelings and experiences change depending on when and how you connect?

The answers to these questions will show you the truths about how you connect, and what kind of relationship you have with the Sacred at this point in your life.

For example, no matter what method I'm using to connect with the Sacred, my experiences are of brightness, clarity and spaciousness. At the very root of my experiences is a feeling of opening and flow, as though I am a river, or a heart that's breaking open with light. What can change is how deeply I connect, how open I am to the flow, and the form that Spirit takes - as an energy, a being, light, sensation or simply a shift in my awareness.

Practice: Dream Work

One other great practice for exploring our connection with the Sacred, one that allows us to ask questions and receive the answers in return, is working with our dreams. Dream work is the practice of using our dreams to interact with the Sacred and our own inner natures, and the simplest form of dream work is just asking a question before we go to sleep and then examining our dreams the next day for the answer that's within them.

To use dream work to find the truth of our connection with the Sacred, you will need to have your journal beside your bed before you go to sleep, together with a pen. Make sure you pick a night when having strong dreams won't be a problem the next day, and when you're unlikely to be disturbed during your sleep.

Before you go to sleep, open sacred space in your favourite way by calling for the Sacred to be with you and to work with you during the night. Breathe deeply for a few moments, becoming aware of the presence of Spirit around you, and thank it for joining you. You can also call for any guides or teachers you are working with to be with you and assist you during your dreams as well.

Clearly state your intent, either out loud, silently or on paper, to be shown a truth about your relationship with the Sacred during your dreams that night. Let go of any expectations or assumptions about how the Sacred may communicate with you, and be open to whatever message or meaning you need to receive. Lie down and go to sleep as usual, leaving sacred space open around you all night.

If you wake at any point during the night, jot down your dreams as clearly and fully as you can before going back to sleep, and do the same in the morning as soon as you wake up. Then close sacred space and go about your day as usual.

Because you wrote down the details of your dreams, they will probably stay fresh in your mind throughout the day. You can also read them over a couple of times, to re-fresh your memory of them. Don't think about them, though; just let them simmer in the back of your mind.

This stage is important in dream work - by letting the dreams 'cook' in you subconscious, you are allowing all of their meaning and symbolism to be de-coded and grounded into your awareness. If you try to make sense of them too quickly, or with too much thought and not enough intuition, you could get frustrated or confused.

Later in the day, take your journal and sit in a quiet space for a little while, reading over your notes on the dream and remembering it as fully as you can. Let any meanings or messages come into your awareness, and note them down in your journal. Notice all the little details that you jotted down - anything with a vivid and specific colour, or any words that were said to you.

Pay attention as well to the location of the dream, and the people in it with you. Many people, when they dream about their relationship with the sacred, dream about their partner - it's common for our partners to represent our more powerful, intimate relationships, which is certainly the kind of relationship that we have with Spirit!

But our dreams are also very individual, and the symbolism and meaning we work with is unique to us and our experiences. Dreams communicate on the level of the soul, speaking in a language of association, metaphor and memory. For example, an elephant could be about something large, obvious and dangerous for one person, and could represent the circus for someone else!

Take all the time you need to de-code the meaning of your dream by letting the symbols float to the surface of your awareness. It can sometimes take days or even months for the meaning of a dream to become clear, so don't feel the need to rush this. And similarly, you may find your dream extremely clear and simple to understand - don't second guess yourself or think that it can't be that easy, either.

These are difficult experiences to put into words, and are often impossible to translate perfectly into coherent sentences. A connection with Spirit is, by its very nature, beyond the mind; it is of soul and heart and energy. But by asking these questions, we turn our focus to the answers; and by doing this, we become familiar with the truth even if we cannot describe it to anyone else.

So don't get hung up on the words - instead, focus on feeling that essence of your relationship with Spirit, and recognising it. Once we know what the truth of our connection with the Sacred is, even if that truth is simply an indescribable feeling, we can let that knowledge work in our lives.

Truth From The Fire

The truth that we can really rely on is the truth which we discover for ourselves. When we take the attitude of a scientist, exploring our own experiences and perceptions, we become empowered to find the truth as it appears to us rather than accept other people's versions of the truth.

Another part of our lives that holds great and deep experiences for us is where we have been wounded or become out of balance. These places within us are rich in truth, hard won through being lived and learnt personally, directly and concretely.

When we allow ourselves to see these experiences from a place of connection, we are able to go beyond the pain or fear to see the beauty of what happened. This process of digging up the truth of your life's experiences is like growing roots - the more you do it, the more truth you have to rely on, and the more stable you will be when the winds of change blow.

By finding these truths, we are able to answer the questions about how life works and what it means for us, what is important to us, and what works and what doesn't work to create a life that we want to live.

The truth that lives in the fire of our challenging experiences has already, in some ways, been found. All that is left for us to do is to recognise it, and integrate it into our lives. And to do this, we have to be willing to really see those experiences, clearly and from a place of connection and healing rather than woundedness. When we can do this, the experiences can transform, showing us a new way of perceiving the world and ourselves, and with it a new understanding of the truths of existence.

To begin unearthing these truths, we must first become comfortable with our connection to the Sacred, because it is this place within us that will give us the power to transform pain into blessings. Once we have a solid relationship with the Sacred, we can bring that energy and vision to our memories and choose to see them differently.

Practice: Choosing Your Truth

You can do this practice as often as you like, perhaps even as part of your daily spiritual routine, or just when you're working through a specific issue. Choose an experience to work with - it can be a pleasant or painful one, it could be from the past or something that you're experiencing right now.

To begin with, sit quietly and connect with the Sacred in the way that works best for you. Allow yourself to relax, letting go of any thoughts or worries from the day. Spend a few minutes just breathing deeply, feeling the space around you and the presence of Spirit.

Then call to mind the experience you have chosen, letting it come to the surface of your awareness. Ask yourself what interpretation you currently have for this experience, and let the answer come to you. Your perception of the experience may surprise you, or you might recognise it as a way of thinking about things that you habitually use.

As an example, imagine that you recently had a car accident that left you mildly injured. Letting this experience come into your awareness, you may realise that, deep down, you feel betrayed and angry that this happened to you, in spite of all your carefulness; your interpretation of the experience could be that the world is a hard and unfair place where bad things happen no matter what you do to avoid them, and this car accident was just another of those unfair things. And you may recognise this way of thinking about life from other situations you've been in, such as when a partner left you, when you got ill or when you didn't win a job that you interviewed for.

The interpretation that you have for the experience might feel true in your heart, or it might not. Let yourself sit with it for a moment and notice how it makes you feel. Then jot down the interpretation and ask yourself what other perspectives could you use to interpret this experience?

At first, look for the most negative interpretation that you can come up with. Once this has come to you, write it down and move on without thinking about it. Now, look for interpretations that feel better. Take your time and allow them to come naturally, then write these down too.

For example, you could interpret a car accident as a 'near miss', and feel grateful that you were taken care of in some way and escaped serious injury. Or you could see the experience as a 'wake up', encouraging you to pay more attention to the important things in your life and to live in a more authentic way. Or you could see the car accident as simply something that had to happen to get you where you need to be in some way, whether that's meeting the friendly doctor at the hospital or not going to work the next day and so missing a bigger, more dangerous accident.

Once you have three or four really good-feeling interpretations stop looking for more and sit with the ones you have. You don't have to think about them, or weigh them up in any way. Remember that your heart is the best tool for finding the truth.

You may find that the interpretations that you discover bring up emotions within you. That's absolutely ok, and why it's important to call on Spirit and your guides before doing this work. This is especially true if you're working on a painful or challenging experience.

As you sit with these new interpretations, tune into your heart and how it's feeling about each of them. One of these ways of looking at your experience will feel right to you - trust that feeling. It won't just be the interpretation that's the most positive - it will be the one that feels absolutely right. It will seem to shine somehow. That's the truth - your heart's truth - about this matter. It maybe the interpretation you began with, or it may be one of the others.

My only guidance would be that if it doesn't feel joyful or relieving or peaceful to you in some way, then your head is probably getting in the way of the process. If this happens, try again at another time when you can focus on your heart more clearly, or use a simple ceremony to release any obstacles to your healing in this area.

The Truth About Who We Are

The most fundamental aggression to ourselves, the most fundamental harm we can do to ourselves, is to remain ignorant by not having the courage and the respect to look at ourselves honestly and gently.
Pema Chödrön, When Things Fall Apart

Just as we can find the truth about Spirit and our experiences, we can also discover the truth about ourselves. Most of us learn, as we grow up, that to be accepted we must present a mask to the world. Every aspect of us that doesn't fit with this mask becomes unacceptable to us - it's no longer ok to be that kind of person, to have that aspect, that face, within us.

This process of splitting off from and rejecting parts of ourselves is well known in psychology, and the parts that we have rejected are known as our Shadow. Our Shadow is our hidden self; the parts of us that, for some reason or another, we learnt we couldn't safely express, and so we deny them – hiding them as deeply as we can, even from ourselves.

This constant denial of our wholeness takes energy, and lots of it. And it means that when we're threatened with the truth about ourselves - when we see that rejected aspect reflected back to us in another person - we feel threatened. It makes us irrational, angry, condescending or afraid, and it makes us judgemental.

When we can discover and accept the truth about who and what we really are, we no longer have to bear these side effects; we have more energy, we're more relaxed, more compassionate and we have all of our power available to us to use and benefit from. And, on top of all those great reasons to reclaim our lost Shadow, we receive another gift - more truth with which to anchor our inner peacefulness during times of change.

A person who is truly comfortable with all of the aspects of themselves, someone who has re-integrated their shadow, is a powerful and stable being indeed. Not only do they have access to all the medicine and power that those rejected parts took with them when they were banished, but they also have the peace of knowing that whoever they choose to be, in whatever situation, they are acceptable; they are able to truly love themselves.

To reclaim our Shadow selves, we have to be able to see them and open ourselves up to working with them. This can be a challenging experience, especially if you've spent a long time repressing and denying lots of parts of yourself, and were taught that those parts are totally unacceptable, ugly or wrong. But the power of our connection to the Sacred doesn't just help us with our relationship to change - it can help us to heal and move forward in every area of our lives, including re-claiming our lost soul parts.

As a fantastic beginning practice that will initiate your shadow journey, a Shadow Altar is a beautiful and gentle way of healing our shadow parts and helping them to re-integrate. As we've already seen, an altar is a symbolic space that allows us to safely work with a specific energy or archetype. By going to our altar regularly, and ceremonially maintaining the space, we create a kind of bubble of Spirit around the altar that contains and heals everything that comes in contact with it.

Practice: The Shadow Altar

To create your Shadow Altar, choose a space that will be private and undisturbed - the inside of a drawer or cupboard can be perfect, as can a bedroom windowsill. The most important thing to consider when choosing an altar space is that it should feel right to you.

When you have your altar space, begin to create your altar by first calling on Spirit to be present there, in the way the works best for you. Make sure that you feel that sacred presence in your altar space before continuing to the next steps. If you find that it's difficult to create the sacred space, or can't find a place that feels right, then consider whether you have any resistance to doing shadow work and ask for help from Spirit and your guides.

Once you have created your sacred space you can begin to build your altar. The Shadow Altar is a place for you to work with your shadow aspects; these are the parts of you that you don't like, are afraid of, can't accept or can't face. So it's natural for your shadow altar to be an uncomfortable place for you at first - the objects that you place on it, and the energies you work with there, are going to challenge you as you do this healing work. Just remember to be gentle with yourself.

Place objects on the altar that symbolise the qualities and parts of yourself that you feel negatively about or don't accept exist within you. For example, you could put red objects to symbolise the anger in you, a toy weapon to symbolise the violence within you, or something broken to represent your wounded or imperfect self.

Again, the important thing to remember when creating your altar is to use objects that have personal associations for you, and feel right in your heart. Simply by recognising these objects and the faces that they represent will illuminate your shadow aspects; through honouring them and allowing their gifts to become apparent you will develop an awareness of the truth of the whole, sacred being that you are.

Arrange your objects in the way that feels right, and spend some time just sitting with your altar, feeling the space. You might like to light a candle or some incense, or to decorate your altar with glitter or herbs to honour the aspects you are working with.

When you feel that your altar is ready, speak your intent to work with and re-integrate your Shadow. You can speak out loud, or silently - what matters is that you are calling on the Sacred and your Shadow aspects to come and work with you in this space.

Leave the sacred space open around your altar for a week, and spend time with it every day. You can bring it gifts, add objects, and move around the objects that you've already arranged on it - remember that the altar is symbolic of your relationship with these parts of yourself, and as your relationship changes your altar might too.

Practice: Calling the Lost Shadow Home

Once you have set up your Shadow Altar, you can begin to call home the parts of yourself that you have lost. Go to your altar and spend a few moments just connecting and relaxing, feeling the space around you and the presence of the Sacred.

When you are ready, call out for your Shadow parts in a similar way to opening sacred space. Ask them to come to the altar and work with you, stating your intent to honour them and their gifts to you. You might also like to ask for support and guidance from your guides and Spirit.

Stay with your altar for a few minutes, noticing any changes in the space, or within you. Emotions and feelings may come to the surface for you to recognise, or you may experience an insight into a particular part of you and how it can help you. Remember to note them down in your journal so that you can work with them later.

Thank these parts of your soul for coming back and being willing to work with you, maybe offering them some incense. Then leave the altar and continue with your day.

As you work with these lost aspects of yourself, you will find that transformations happen in both your outer and inner lives. Be open to these changes, and know that they are the result of a deep healing process that is returning your lost power and life energy to you.

Developing Heart Knowing

Throughout the first section, I invited you to pay attention to what your heart was telling you. This knowledge that comes from deep within us is our heart knowing; the innate wisdom of our souls. Through this knowing, we can directly discover the truth as it appears to us, through experiencing it within ourselves. And while this can sound a bit strange, or like 'making it up', it can be extremely effective and practical for making personal decisions and making sense of our lives in a way that really works for us.

When we are able to access this inner knowing we can find our truth in any situation; we can discover healing, create practical solutions and empower ourselves to find the way through life that is best for us. This is because, deep inside all of us, we know everything that Spirit knows - we are connected, and every question that we ask has an answer that we can understand, if we can only allow ourselves to hear it.

When we can access this ability during times of change, we become able to find answers to the most pressing questions quickly and reliably. The answers we find will always be what we need at the time, and will guide us through the changes that are going on around us in the best way possible, because they come from our most sacred, knowing selves, the parts of us that know exactly what we need and how to get it. When we can listen to these parts of ourselves, we become free to self-reference - to source the meaning of our lives from within, rather than relying on second-hand meanings that have been given to us by others.

To develop this ability to hear the wisdom of our hearts, we have to listen for it. Our daily spiritual practice is a great time to do this, because every time we connect with the Sacred, we are also connected with this power to know the truth. Two great, daily practices that we can use to develop this awareness are mindfulness and journeying. Each provides a different way for us to allow the truth to be recognised and understood; mindfulness, through watching our own reactions and feelings about things and using them as signposts to the underlying truth, and journeying as a way of allowing the truth to speak to us in a way that we can personally understand. Both of these methods are extremely powerful, and through using them your ability to discern truth will develop quickly.

But we can also develop this ability to feel the truth by using it in our everyday lives - asking ourselves how we feel about a person, conversation, choice or experience as we go about our day, and listening for the honest answer. When we first begin to do this it can take a few minutes for us to 'tune in' to what our inner wisdom is saying. But as we practice, it becomes easier and quicker, until we are able to hear the guidance that we need with just a few moments of focusing.

Practice: Listening to the Heart

To begin with, we have to practice finding and recognising the guidance of our hearts so that we can reliably access this inner wisdom when we need it, without having to think about it. Aside from using practices like mindfulness and journeying, we can take a few moments out of our day to specifically connect with our heart-knowing as a practice in itself.

At first, you might find it useful to go somewhere that you won't be disturbed. You could go and sit in a garden or a park, take a seat in a church, or even make yourself comfortable in a bathroom - anywhere that you feel comfortable and safe, so that you can focus inwardly for a few minutes.

Take three or four slow, gentle breaths, letting yourself relax with each exhale. You can close your eyes if you like, or listen to music through some earphones if that helps you. As you breathe, turn your focus inward; allow the world around you to fall away until you are very clearly aware of your internal state - your feelings and thoughts.

Find the still centre, or heart, of that inner world, and let yourself see or feel or hear or simply know what is held there. You don't need to 'do' anything to find this place within you, simply allow yourself to become aware of it. If it would help you, you could state your intent to connect with your inner knowing, either out loud or silently, or you could imagine yourself sinking down into it within your body.

Ask yourself a couple of questions that you already know the answer to, like 'do I love my family?' or 'do I work at such & such a place?' and be open to receive the answer. You might hear it, or see it, or simply feel it, but it will be recognisable and very clear to you.

Once you feel that you've connected with this place, let it go and begin to return to your everyday awareness. Allow your senses and your mind to return to normal, knowing that the still, peaceful place of inner wisdom will always be within you.

When beginning this practice, it's often best to stick to answers that will have a yes or no answer to them, as these are the most simple and reliable answers you can get. Try not to think about what you're feeling or hearing, and don't second guess yourself - if the answer isn't clear, or you're not comfortable with it, you can try asking the question in another way, or leave it until later.

Often, if we ask a question that has a particularly strong emotion attached to it, like 'what are the winning lottery numbers?' or 'is my partner cheating on me?', the answers that we get are muddied or unclear, and sometimes we won't get an answer at all. This is because we are blocking our inner knowledge with our attachment to a particular answer, and it shows how important it is to calm ourselves and connect with the Sacred before we begin to work with our Heart-Knowing.

Similarly, if we ask for information about someone else without permission we will get either unclear answers or no answers at all. It's important to keep our questions to ourselves and the issues in our own lives, so if you are working with an issue that involves someone else, keep your questions to you, your actions, your perceptions and feelings, and what's right for you in the situation. This way, we keep within our integrity, which is essential for our own well being, and avoid creating disharmony in our relationships.

Practice: Dowsing With The Heart

Once we are comfortable connecting with our inner knowing and asking basic, 'yes or no' questions, we can begin to apply this practice to the situations we come across in our daily lives. We can do this practice at any time, for any reason - we can use it to ask how to mend an argument, or which book to buy, or who to call first, or how to get better from a cold quicker, or where our lost wallet is.

To begin with, find a calm, quiet place that you feel comfortable in, and connect to your heart in the way that you did before. Once you are fully aware of that still place inside you, bring to mind the situation or question you want to ask about, letting it become clear and present for you. Often, before you have even asked your question you will find that an answer is coming to you - let it come, and trust what you feel or hear.

Your inner self knows the answer to every question that is important to you, and as you practice listening to its voice the guidance you receive will become clearer and more relevant.

Take a few moments to allow the answer to unfold, and then shift your focus back to your surroundings and your body. Let your mind return to its normal awareness, and give the answer you discovered some space to settle into your consciousness so that you can interpret and integrate it fully. You might like to give thanks for the answers, or to say a prayer before you go about the rest of your day - you've just been given a little sacred insight to help you on you path!

Calling on our inner wisdom is something that we can all do, no matter what our spiritual path or how we see ourselves. As we practice listening to and trusting our personal guidance, it becomes easier to hear the voice of our hearts. So don't be disheartened if, at first, you can't hear a clear answer, or if you find that sometimes it's easier and other times it's harder. Over time, your awareness of this other side of yourself will grow.

Through learning how to discover the truth for ourselves, we free ourselves to decide what is important, what is helpful, what is healing and what is beautiful in our lives. We become able to withstand change in the outer world without losing sight of those important, nourishing foundations, and we can relax in the knowledge that no matter what changes or disappears, we know how to find the truths that matter to us, and we know who we are, wherever we are.

Don't worry if this ongoing process of discovering your truth brings up emotions for you. This is, after all, a personal process aimed at increasing your empowerment, peace and well-being; it's natural to occasionally come across old issues, wounds and outdated maps that have been holding you back.

Know that as you bring your connection with the Sacred to these challenges, they will be transformed within you to reveal even more truth with which you can ground your life. The shift may be quick, or it may be more subtle, depending on what you need at the time, what you are ready for, and how deeply you are working with your spiritual practices.

But trust that as you choose to move forward and empower yourself more and more, Spirit and your soul will support you and guide you, and you will discover beautiful truths that set you free to live the life you dream of. Keep practising and keep connecting, and don't forget to ask for help from Spirit, your guides, your loved ones and professionals if needed.

Section Four:

Courage

Courage of the soul takes us beyond petty human emotions and lets us live authentically, speaking our truth and breaking the rules even when it's embarrassing or uncomfortable to do so.
Alberto Villoldo, Courageous Dreaming

The word courage means 'the ability to do something that frightens one' or 'strength in the face of pain or grief'. In Middle English, 'courage' was used to denote the heart as the seat of feelings, and it is related to the Latin word 'cor', which means 'heart'.

The heart is the centre, the core, the essence; symbolically, it is through the heart that we love, feel and connect with others and with Spirit. And as we learnt in the previous section, through our hearts we are also able to access great inner wisdom and the deepest truths of our souls. So it's no wonder that courage, the power to face and do what frightens us, is associated with the heart.

To connect with the Sacred, allowing ourselves to be open and authentic, requires courage. It can be frightening to begin something new, to acknowledge that we need to grow and learn new skills, to make mistakes and to accept new ideas. It can be challenging to feel and perceive in a new way, and to learn to trust in something beyond our minds.

Similarly, courage also allows us to find and trust our own, inner truths, by giving us the strength to listen to our own hearts over the opinions and desires of others. Taking responsibility for choosing what to accept as the truth, facing up to the pain of mistakes we've made and the places where we've been hurt, and choosing to accept our lost shadow parts, which bring us so much strength and personal power, all take courage.

And to make a journey of personal exploration or healing requires courage - the power and motivation of our hearts. If we aren't able to access the courageousness that lives within us, we become frozen, unable to act and unable to feel anything beyond our fear.

Courage allows us to make a commitment to our own well being, and everything that will contribute to that. It allows us to face changes in the moment without freezing up or become overwhelmed, to take responsibility for ourselves and our lives, and ultimately to envision something new when opportunities arise for us to change the world around us.

So courage is hugely important for dealing with our fears of change and learning to thrive in a changing world. When we learn to grow our own courage, we become able to face the changes around us while remaining free to choose what is best for us. We can commit to the practices that help us to thrive, even when they challenge us to face the things that scare us, and we can take responsibility for doing what we know is best for us.

Often, personal traits and characteristics are considered as things that we either have or don't have. We tend to define ourselves by our abilities, describing ourselves as confident, organized, nervous or generous as though these things are set in stone. But our abilities are all subject to change; they are fluid expressions of who we are. We are able to choose which aspects to act on, and to strengthen those that are most helpful to us.

So just as we can practice connecting with the Sacred, we can practice expressing our courage. The practices in this section will help you to do just that, and while some may be challenging to you, these are the ones that will hold the most power and effectiveness for you personally.

Developing Courage through Practising Courage

Courage, like connection and truth, is something that is always within each of us - it just needs a little practice to help bring it to the surface. And growing courage, just like growing our ability to connect with the Sacred and our awareness of our inner wisdom, requires that we use our courage, giving ourselves the opportunity discover for ourselves how we experience and work with fear in our own, unique, way.

Practice: Commitment To Courage Ceremony

To make a commitment to something means choosing to fulfil our intent about it - we make a commitment to our partners when we enter a relationship, we make a commitment to our jobs when we sign our contracts, and we make commitments to our children when they are born. In each of these, our intent is to meet the requirements of the situation, and when we choose to fulfil that intent, to actually do what we've said we'll do, we are committing ourselves to that situation.

Making a commitment takes courage. It can be frightening to stick with something, even though we don't know where it will take us. It can be daunting to undertake a course of action that we don't know we can complete, a course that will require our deepest strength. And it can be worrying to be faced with making a commitment when we have failed to meet a previous one, or feel that we've let ourselves down in some way before.

A ceremony of intent, like the one we did at the beginning of this book, is a commitment ceremony. We are telling ourselves and the world what our intent is, and that we are ready to fulfil it, and we are asking for support from the Sacred in our journey towards accomplishing that intent. Part of the reason why ceremonies are so powerful is that they rally all of our inner and outer resources towards the fulfilment of our intent, committing us to our actions and setting us on the course we've chosen to take.

So it seems important, now, to begin our work on courage with a commitment ceremony. You can use whichever of the ceremonies described earlier to create your commitment ceremony, or you can use the one described below, depending on how you feel and which types of ceremony work best for you. If the one below doesn't feel right, or you don't have access to a body of water, you could hold a prayer ceremony, or a commitment walk, or even a community ceremony where you state your intent to your friends and family, or simply give your offering to the earth - whatever feels right to you.

The power of ceremony is in your intent, and the amount of energy, or effort, you put into it. Ceremonies can shift the most difficult inner barriers, when we put the work into them. And by work, I mean the time and thought to choose the most effective form of ceremony for us, and the specific symbolism that will create the desired effect, as well as taking the time to focus your intent so that it is clear and strong when you begin.

Whichever ceremony you decide on, the intent we are working with is to call up our most courageous selves to aid us in the work of this section of the book, and to grow within us as we move forward on our journey with change.

For this simple Commitment To Courage Ceremony, you will need:

- a small offering, such as a feather or a piece of paper
- access to a river, lake or the sea

Choose a day a little in advance to allow you to prepare for your ceremony. Gather a small offering, such as a feather, a piece of paper, flowers, a small piece of food or a glass of wine. Make sure that your offering resonates for you, and wrap it up in a small piece of cloth or a light scarf.

The night before your ceremony, take the wrapped up offering and lay it beside your bed, or even beneath your pillow, before you go to sleep. Before you lie down, tell your intent to the offering, either out loud or silently, or use your breath to blow your intent into it. Tell it that you are calling on your courageous self to come and work with you, and thank it for holding your prayers and wishes. Finally, go to sleep as usual, knowing that as you sleep your deeper awareness will be working with your intent.

The next day, take some time out of your day to visit the water. Stand beside it, as close as you can get, and take a few moments to relax and feel the world around you. Call in your favourite way for the Sacred to be with you, and ask any other guides that you have been working with to come and hold space with you too.

Take a deep breath and hold up your offering. Blow your intent into it again, pouring out all of your longing for courage and strength, the power to act and to do what you need to do no matter the situation. Unwrap your offering from the piece of material, and give thanks to the river, lake or sea as you allow the offering to fall into the water.

Turn away as your offering is accepted, allowing it to be received without attachment and letting go of the outcome - simply know that your prayer has been heard and will be answered appropriately.

Enjoy the presence of the Sacred around you, and give thanks for being able to make this request. And then, when you are ready, close sacred space and return to your day.

Practice: Taking Responsibility - Working with Stones

One of the times that we exercise courage in our lives is when we take responsibility for ourselves. Responsibility is the ability or power to take control over something, as well as the obligation to take decisions and act on them. Taking responsibility for ourselves means to accept the ways that we have created the situations we're in, to recognise the contributions that we make to our own emotions, perceptions and suffering, and to choose actions that serve our own well being.

Responsibility requires courage because it means that we have to face up to our own mistakes and failings, as well as requiring effort of us to do those things that are best for us. It can be frightening to see how we have contributed to even the most painful experiences of our lives, and it can be terrifying to let go of the blame and anger that has prevented us from accepting control of ourselves and what happens to us. It takes compassion to see ourselves in this clear way without blaming or becoming angry with ourselves, and compassion takes courage - it takes the strength of our hearts to resist the temptation to give up on ourselves, or to make things worse with negative thinking. And it takes the power of our connection and courage to keep moving forward with our lives in the direction that we know is best for us, despite previous failures or challenges.

Taking responsibility for ourselves is often a long, slow process. It can take years to re-claim our personal power in every area of our lives, but we can do it - through becoming mindful of when and how we are giving our power, and our responsibility, away, and then choosing differently. To begin this process and work with responsibility as a practice in courage, we can to start looking for the times in our past where we have given away our power and refused to take responsibility for ourselves.

Most of us have had times in our lives that bring up anger or bitterness within us when we remember them. It could have been a relationship that ended badly, or a business project that got taken over by someone else, or it could have been a car accident that left you injured. These kinds of situations are the times when we are most likely to let go of our power and believe that someone else is responsible for our pain - because, of course, no one wants to feel that they were even part of the reason that they suffered, or that there was a reason for that suffering.

But by rejecting our responsibility at times like these, we leave ourselves stuck in the past - if we had no control then, in that situation, then we can't claim our power to influence the world around us now either. If we believe that we were powerless then, we won't be able to accept that we have any power now. And so we can't move on - always giving our power away to avoid the pain of responsibility for causing ourselves suffering, we are trapped in that position of suffering and are powerless to stop it happening again.

To move forward and free ourselves of this catch-22, we have to use courage. When we are able to connect with our hearts and trust what we find there, using the support of the Sacred and our ability to know the truth when we see it, we can re-claim the power we lost and take responsibility for our lives again - allowing us to choose differently, and take an active part in forming the world around us.

A wonderful practice for working with past experiences, and so reclaiming our responsibility, is working with Stones. Stones are the great masters of holding and processing energies, and through their deep connection with the earth they are very good at transforming painful or unhelpful emotions into more helpful, healed energies. In the shamanic tradition, stones are considered beings in their own right, with spirits and powers of their own which we can call on to help and support us in our healing.

To do this practice, you will need:

- a stone, small enough to be carried comfortably in your hand
- a place outside where you can leave your stone overnight

Choose a stone that resonates with you and with the experience you want to work with, and let your heart guide you in your choice. Trust what you feel - you will know the right one when you see it.

Once you have chosen your stone, you are going to give all of your feelings and memories about this past experience to it so that it can help you transform them and find the truth of your own power within them. This may sound strange, but it's actually very simple - through holding and mulching the energy of your memory, the stone will then be able to give back to you the core of the experience so that you can perceive it in a new, clearer, more empowered way.

Choose a time when you are relaxed and able to connect easily. Call upon the Sacred in the way that works best for you, and allow yourself a few moments to become aware of it's presence around you.

Then, when you are ready, call to mind a time in your past when you were hurt, a time that brings up feelings of anger, blame or bitterness for you. Allow the experience to come to the surface of your awareness, and let yourself be with it for a few moments. Use your mindfulness and awareness of the space to notice how the memory makes you feel, what thoughts your mind has about it, and how your body feels as you think about it.

Then, take a deep breath and blow all of these thoughts, feelings and sensations into the stone. Let yourself become empty of the old memories, giving them to the stone and asking for them to be transformed. Tell the stone, either silently or out loud, that you want to take responsibility for your part in what happened, and to be free to reclaim the power you lost at that time.

When you feel that you've blown all of your feelings into the stone, place it in the space you have chosen and ask for the Sacred to be with it, similar to when we create altar spaces and sandpaintings.

Leave your stone for a week and let it work. You can spend time with it if you like, or you can simply leave it alone until you're ready to go back. Know that as your stone works with your memory of the experience, you may find that feelings and ideas come up in your awareness, or in your dreams, or that you have insights into the experience that you've never had before. This is perfectly normal, and simply shows that the practice is working for you.

When the week is up, go back to your stone. It may have moved a little, or even vanished! Don't worry about this - just be in the space for a little while, re-connecting with the Sacred and becoming open to the new perceptions you have been given.

Thank the stone for its work with you, picking it up if it's still there, and ask it to give you the truth about your experience. Take some time to allow this new perception to settle into you - it may be conscious, or you may not feel anything at all, just trust that a new perception of the event is now in your awareness.

You may like to ask the stone how you made the experience possible. Allow yourself some time to receive the answer, and be open to the various ways that the Sacred can communicate with you. You might see the answer, or hear it spoken in words, or simply get a feeling - allow it all to come to you and know that it will make sense over time.

Close the Sacred Space in the way that works best for you, giving thanks for this new knowledge and the opportunity to reclaim your power. If the stone was still there and it feels right to do so, thank it and take it with you so that you can work with it again, or leave it somewhere that feels appropriate.

Practice: Standing In Our Integrity - A Practice In Saying No

Having integrity means being honest, having strong principles, being whole, being strongly constructed, being consistent and being without corruption. It is about your actions matching your truth and the nature of your soul.

And integrity takes courage. To stand firm in your truth in the face of opposition takes the strength of our hearts; to say what we mean, to do what is best for our own wholeness and well being, and to remain true to our inner natures can be frightening and even painful if we are under pressure to give in to others, or tempted to discard our own knowing because it's harder to live with.

But when we can live with integrity, we have an inner wholeness that gives us power - the power to be who we are, communicate our truths clearly and authentically, and create lives that really serve our best interests rather than being swayed by what is popular, 'normal' or fashionable.

In times of change, having integrity means that we stand with what we know is right and true for us, giving us a reliable and constant way of understanding the world, and our own actions. A person with integrity will stand by their principles, even if that means they experience a temporary challenge, rather than giving in to fear and persuasion that will ultimately lead to confusion about who they are, what they stand for and what is important in their lives. They maintain their inner power, instead of giving it up in exchange for the easy solution that will get them no where.

Integrity, just like all the other personal powers in this book, is something that we can only build through practice. When we use our integrity by choosing to do what is consistent with our inner natures and resisting the temptation to do something that betrays our own truths, we develop more power to choose and to act appropriately. And in doing so, we are also exercising our ability to be courageous.

The courage that allows us to have integrity can be thought of as strength - just as a bridge or a building needs strength to have structural integrity, we must use the strength that comes from our experiences, and the knowledge that we have gained through them, to guide our decisions and choices, and to support us in upholding them.

A wonderful practice for building this kind of strength is saying 'no'. Many of us find it hard to say no to others, and even to ourselves. We begin to learn this when we are little, learning that to say no is to create disagreement, conflict and resentment, and that to say yes fosters affection, praise and appreciation - it's easy to see how we can develop a habit of only saying yes.

But this habit is often unhelpful to our well being, causing us to say yes to things that we would really be better off not doing, and agreeing to opinions that don't resonate with out own truths. We betray ourselves in the process and end up causing all sorts of problems such as fatigue, depression, resentment and misunderstanding in relationships, stress at work, and a loss of understanding of who we are and what is important to us.

Being able to say no means that we can choose freely - deciding for ourselves what is best for us, what is true for us, and what is important for us. It also means that when we say yes, we can really mean it, allowing us to give our best to our work, our relationships and to our lives in general.

To use saying no as a practice in courage and integrity, begin slowly and be gentle with yourself. Maybe once a day, or once a week, make it a practice to say no to a request that you're not comfortable with.

When you are asked to contribute your time or resources in some way, take your time to decide how you need to answer, listening to your inner knowing and paying attention to how the request makes you feel in your heart. Just being able to give yourself this time to assess the situation is an act of courage and integrity, and people will appreciate your authenticity and the respect you are giving to them in truly considering the situation rather than answering by habit.

Once you have acknowledged all of your feelings and understanding of the situation, give them your answer with certainty and clarity. This can take courage, especially if the person is someone very important to you, or someone who often exerts authority over you, but remember as you do it that you're building courage and personal power. If it helps you, you could connect with the Sacred before you give your answer, or ask for guidance on the situation from your guides while you consider the request.

Once you are more comfortable with doing this, you can begin to assess every request that is made to you. Being able to truly and honestly respond to everyone in your life is an empowering thing, and you'll find that as you do so your perception of yourself, and of other people, will begin to shift - becoming more compassionate, calm and authentic.

Developing Discipline in our Practice - Acts of Power

Discipline is the ability to choose our actions based on our inner knowledge, and our commitment to what is best for us. It allows us to keep practising, keep trying, keep learning, keep striving for new experiences and understanding, even when it might be easier to choose a less challenging, less conscious path in our lives.

Discipline is associated with learning and training, such as an 'academic discipline', a 'physical discipline', and 'spiritual disciplines' like meditation. While it is often associated with punishment and control of behaviour, the personal power of discipline is actually one of individual strength and the freedom to choose how we live our lives, free from both external and internal distractions.

When we have discipline, we become able to follow a path of practice and growth - to move forward in our lives, developing new abilities, reclaiming old parts of ourselves, and becoming more peaceful and powerful in the world as it changes around us.

Without discipline, we cannot consistently continue the practises that help us. When we become distracted, resistant and doubtful, we have no strength to bring us back to the path we have chosen. We become disconnected from our relationship to the Sacred and our own, inner knowing, and we lack the will and the power to use the practices that we know will help us to regain our connection and move forward.

So discipline is an important personal power to develop, and one that strengthens our ability to be courageous at the same time. Through practising being disciplined, we can exercise our courageous selves, that aspect of us that is determined, focused and undeterred by setbacks and challenges.

To begin developing discipline, we can use it to stick to a new routine, such as a connection practice like meditation or journalling, or to break an old habit like smoking or unhelpful patterns of thinking. Both of these are acts of power - actions that we take with the intent of reclaiming personal power.

Practice: Creating a Routine

Before you begin, take some time to think about what you'd like to achieve - do you want to connect more deeply with an aspect of your spirituality, to increase your level of physical well being, access your inner creativity, become more skilful at a particular spiritual practice, or work towards healing an old wound that is holding you back. Whatever your aim, keep that in mind as you craft your new routine, remembering that it's our intent that fuels our progress.

Once you know what you'd like to achieve, decide what new practice will be most helpful in creating that effect for you. If you've done some exploring of how you work best with the Sacred, you'll know some core practices that really get results, but you don't have to use something you're familiar with. Instead, you can always choose a new practice, to keep the attitude of exploration fresh, or you can let your heart decide on the best practice for you at this time, noticing how each idea for your routine feels to you and letting those feelings guide you.

Pay close attention to how you feel as you create your new routine. It's important to approach this as a practice, rather than as a way of punishing ourselves - there's nothing more unhelpful than setting ourselves an impossible goal and then feeling bad about ourselves when we give up trying to reach it! Instead, focus on stretching yourself just outside of your 'comfort zone' by choosing a practice and type of routine that is only a little bit more challenging that something you've done previously.

For example, if you've been sitting down to meditate for 10 minutes every day as part of your daily connection practice, you might think about increasing that time to 20 minutes rather than a whole hour, or you could add 10 minutes of another practice such as yoga, dancing or journalling to complement your meditation. In this way, we give ourselves the opportunity to succeed, and reclaim our power and courage as we do so, realising that we can achieve what we set out to do.

It's also important to give yourself a time frame to work within. Deciding to do half an hour of painting every day may be very helpful for your creativity, but if there's no end date for your decision you might get easily downhearted or doubtful. Instead of leaving your routine open ended, give yourself a set number of days, weeks or months to practice within.

For example, you could decide to do a shamanic journey once a week for a month, and see how you feel when that month is up. Or you could set a routine of 5 minutes of light exercise three times a day for one week. This will allow you to adjust your routine as you go along without feeling guilty, and will prevent you from feeling overwhelmed by the task you've chosen.

The most important thing to remember when creating a routine in this way is to pay close attention to how your idea feels to you. Like other practices where we challenge ourselves in order to develop personal power, your routine may not feel comfortable to you at first, but if it is authentic and truly in your best interests it will feel right.

Courage Through Knowledge

"...he asked me what healing was, and I told him that it was reaching peace, which was freedom from fear."
Fools Crow

Another way in which we can develop courage is through gaining knowledge of fear and of ourselves. This is because to develop a deeper understanding of fear, we must face it, so that when we come to face it again we are more practised, we know what we are dealing with, and we have an awareness of what works for us and what doesn't when we're feeling afraid.

Facing and learning about our fears also helps us to develop courage because it gives us the opportunity to practice using our courage - it can be frightening to even think about those things that scare us, or to look at the parts of ourselves, our mistakes and weaknesses, that we find hard to accept. By exercising the courage required to do these practices, we strength our ability to show courage in other situations, because we already know that we have that inner resource to draw on, and where to find it within us.

To develop our knowledge in a way that helps us become more courageous, we must explore what makes us fearful - our shadow selves, our failures, our successes, our vulnerabilities and even fear itself. These are the places that truly scare us, and accordingly, they are the place where we have the most opportunity to re-discover our power, strength and courage.

When you're using these practices, be gentle with yourself. Bring a compassionate attitude to yourself and others, and know that just doing this work and being willing to even consider examining your fears takes courage in and of itself.

Practice: Knowing Fear

Fear can take many forms, from mild anxiety to paralysing terror. And surprisingly, we can be just as afraid of the good stuff as the bad, sometimes more so; if we do begin to find out the truth for ourselves, we might have to change our perceptions and even our behaviour. If we reclaim our power and take responsibility for ourselves, we might have to let go of all the old excuses and reasons why we're unhappy, and begin to make different choices.

How you experience fear may be different to how your partner, your parents, your friends or your neighbours experience fear. Like all other internal states, it's deeply personal and unique to us. Where one person finds the thumping heart and rushing blood of adrenalin exciting, another finds it overwhelming. Respecting these differences, and coming to know our individual way of experiencing things, is part of developing our own way of living in the world.

A powerful practice for learning about fear and how it feels, is to illicit the feeling on purpose. This is a practice that takes courage, trust in the Sacred and ourselves, and awareness. But as we develop the ability to consciously face our fear, looking it in the eye and really finding out what it is, we develop not only our courage but also our familiarity with it so that when we're confronted by fear at another time, we already know what to expect.

Creating a sensation of fear is something that is best done in very small doses, with planning and care. I'm certainly not recommending that you do anything that could actually harm you, but only that you take just one step closer to the things that frighten you than you usually would.

To begin working with fear in this way you could look at a picture of what scares you, such as a spider, an avalanche, a fire or a weapon. You might like to open sacred space before you begin the practice, or to ask for support from your guides. Take some time to sit with the image and notice how you feel. Allow yourself to react to it, letting the fear come up for you, but don't engage with it - don't try and talk yourself out of the feeling, to rationalise it, or to get caught up in scenarios that involve the thing you fear actually happening to you personally. The intent with this practice is simply to create a slight feeling of unease and then to notice what that feels like.

When you're finished, put away the image and take a few deep breaths, letting the adrenalin fade away as you come back to a normal state. If you feel the need, connect with the Sacred in your favourite way, and spend some time enjoying that connection and nourishing yourself with it. When you're ready, pick up your journal and jot down some notes about what you experienced, then go back to your day.

This is a powerful practice, an act of power in itself, and one that you need not do very often. Rather, use it occasionally to remind yourself of the sensation of calm that lies at the heart of fear, once you learn how to observe rather than engage with it.

Practice: Knowing What We Fear

It's difficult to practice courage if we can't acknowledge what it is that we're afraid of. Knowing our fears is hugely important; each one has a gift for us, a gift of power for our lives. And being able to face and recognise our fears means that, even in the midst of change, we will know when fear is influencing us and distorting our perception of the world around us.

And yet, looking at our fears is something that so many of us will avoid at any cost. Many of us are taught that to admit to our fears is to show weakness or vulnerability, and that by paying attention to our fears we can actually make them happen. And while it certainly can happen that dwelling on the things that frighten us can attract those kinds of situations into our lives, this is very different from consciously observing and becoming aware of our fears and how they manifest within us.

So spending a little time to become familiar with our fears is a great practice for developing courage and becoming more able to deal with change. Simply by sitting down with our journal and writing honestly about the things that scare us and why can be very illuminating, and when we come to our fears within a sacred space we bring the healing of our relationship with the Sacred to them as well.

Begin by taking half an hour to sit with your journal, choosing a time when you're rested and unlikely to be disturbed. Create a sacred space by calling on the Sacred to be with you, and spend a few moments to settle into the space and turn your focus inward.

When you're ready to begin, write down the following questions and allow the answers to come to you in their own time. You may find that situations and experiences come up for you that surprise you, or that you can't immediately see the relevance in them. In other cases, the meaning may be obvious - especially if you have an overt phobia or have had a frightening experience.

Just be open to what you're feeling and perceiving, and allow the answers to unfold over time. In some cases, it may take a few days for the meaning to become clear.

- What is the most frightening dream you ever had as a child?
- What is the most scary film you've ever seen, or the scariest book you've ever read?
- What is the worst thing that could ever happen to you?

Let the answers to these questions come to you, paying attention to how each situation feels and any specific details that strike you. Write down some notes for each of them, and then look for any themes or similarities in your answers, similar to the way we work with dreams.

For example, my scariest childhood dream was of an invisible hand that took away my family, and the most frightening film I've seen was about an invisible demon that terrorised a couple. These answers have a theme of invisible, non-physical things having an effect on the physical, everyday world, as well as the sense of powerlessness against a force that cannot be seen or understood. Knowing this has helped me to analyse why I'm scared of the things I'm scared of, and to work with those fears towards reclaiming my power and medicine in the face of those things.

When you have finished interpreting your answers, close your journal and take a few deep, long breaths, exhaling slowly. Release any tension or adrenalin that you've been holding as you do the practice, and give yourself permission to relax again. You might like to spend a few minutes doing a connection practice that works well for you, to help you to access your more open, joyful self again.

When you're ready, close the sacred space, thanking Spirit for being with you and guiding you in the exploration of your fears, and then return to your day.

Practice: Knowing Ourselves

Only when we know our own darkness well can we be present with the darkness of others. Compassion becomes real when we recognize our shared humanity.
Pema Chödrön, The Places That Scare You

Another place in our lives where we can find our fears in order to face them, and so develop our courage, is in ourselves. Earlier in this book, we looked at our Shadows and how they can hide the truth about our whole selves. Looking at our Shadows aspects, working with them and finding their gifts takes courage, and lots of it.

And so does examining our mistakes, weaknesses and

failures. It can feel very unnatural to choose to look at those times in our lives where we liked ourselves the least, but all of these experiences hold power and healing for us that we won't be able to integrate unless we have the courage to search for them.

When we choose to face these memories and perceptions of ourselves, we develop our ability to act in the face of fear, both by exercising the courage needed to examine ourselves in this way, and by developing an awareness of who we truly are, learning to trust and rely on ourselves in a way that will give us strength in the face of any change or challenge.

The Shadow Altar practice that we used in Section 3 is a wonderful way to develop courage - by spending time with our Shadow parts, getting to know them and working to accept them, we are using all the power of our hearts. As an addition to this work, we can use journalling to increase our awareness of our unacceptable aspects, weaknesses and failures as part of developing our courageous selves.

To begin this journalling practice, open sacred space, calling on the Sacred to join you and support you. Sit for a little while as you become aware of the presence of Spirit, perhaps grounding yourself with a visualisation exercise, and becoming fully centred in your connection.

When you are ready, pick up your journal and write down the below questions, then put down your pen. Allow the answers to come to you, just like in the Knowing Your Fears practice - letting any memories, thoughts or feelings rise to the surface of your awareness gently and in their own time. Again, it may take a few minutes for you to get clear answers to the questions, and the answers you receive could be immediately meaningful to you, or it may take a few days to become aware of their full significance. Just be open to the answers you receive, noticing any specific details or emphasis as they unfold.

- Who is the person you dislike the most, and what it is that you dislike about them?

- What would be the worst favour a friend could ask you to do for them?
- What is your most embarrassing or shameful memory?

As in the previous practice, allow the answers to form in your mind and then jot them down quickly. Don't think about them, or begin to argue with yourself about whether they're the right answers - if they come up, they're the right ones for you to work with at this time.

Keeping your answers in your mind, notice any themes, similarities or differences, and note those down as well. Then let them go, closing your journal and releasing any tension or thoughts you might be having about the experience.

Take some time to re-connect with the Sacred and enjoy the sacred space around you, and thank Spirit and your guides for being with you as you do this powerful work. Once you're feeling centred, connected and calm, close sacred space and return to your day.

Don't think too hard about these exercises and the answers that you get from them - they're designed to bring deeply buried memories and experiences into your awareness so that they can be seen and recognised, but the power in the exercise comes from the initial intent, the moments of recognition, and the exercise of courage in being willing to even look at these questions within us. There's no need to try to resolve or 'fix' them, but if you find that you have a strong reaction to them you might consider bringing them to your other practices, such as altar work and ceremony to help address them from a deeper, energetic level rather than simply with your mind.

And remember how important it is to take care of ourselves when we're working at this deep level. Take the time after each practice to connect with the Sacred and nourish yourself from that connection, as well as to ground yourself back into your daily life once the practice is finished.

And if you find the exercises too painful, or that they affect the rest of your day too much, or even if they just don't feel right to you, remember that we must all be guided first and foremost by our own feelings and heart. If you're not ready, or in the right mood, to do these practices, then leave them till later and focus more on developing your relationship with the Sacred and finding your truth, both of which will also gently develop and grow your power of courage.

Working With Courage In Daily Life

Now that we've reconnected with our courage in the comfort of our sacred spaces, it's time to take it out into the world and use it in real life situations. While exercising our courage in everyday interactions and situations is different to practising it at home, doing this is still a practice - by calling up our courage when faced with the small fears of our everyday lives, we are building up the personal power to use it in even more frightening situations, like when we're faced with big changes in the wider world.

And practising courage when we most need it also develops a greater level of trust in our abilities, integrity and strength, meaning that if the time comes when we are deeply challenged, we know that we have the inner resources not just to survive, but to thrive. In a way, practising courage in our daily lives is a rehearsal - teaching us how our own courage feels, how it works and the strategies we can use to make courage more accessible for us in the moments that we need it.

Practice: Working With Resistance - Achieving Old Goals

"Don't stop! It's like life. You just cannot stop because things did not go your way."
Masaaki Hatsumi & Benjamin Cole, Understand? Good. Play!

Resistance is the inner force that holds us back: the part of us that refuses to accept our own development and growth, and works to counteract our work towards it. It is the self-sabotage that we can all be affected by sometimes when we're trying to achieve something beautiful or meaningful, and it gets in the way of our creativity, our passions, our health, our success, our spiritual growth, and our journey towards being able to thrive during times of change.

Resistance comes from our fears - those deeply buried parts of us that are afraid of our own light, energy and divinity, of succeeding, of taking responsibility for ourselves, of our power and of our love. When we choose to reach for greater well being and connection, we will inevitably run up against some kind of resistance at some point, giving us another opportunity to develop our courage.

Through facing and working through our resistance, keeping going when a part of us is screaming for us to turn back and hide, we develop a strength of will and a steadiness of vision that allows us to keep going when other, more frightening challenges are coming our way. And by working through our resistance, we become more able to practice those things which will help us to reclaim our power and face change with ease.

Working with resistance is similar to working with discipline - it requires that we make a conscious choice to follow a course of action, no matter what inner doubts or fears pop up for us. A good practice for developing courage with regard to resistance is the Acts of Power practice we used earlier. Acts of Power require that we move past our resistance so that we can achieve our goals, and every act that we succeed with increases our power to set aside our fears and choose what's best for us instead.

When we were working with discipline towards developing our power of courage, we used acts of power to create a daily routine that encouraged us to keep going even when we wanted to give up, working through our resistance to creating a new habit or breaking an old one.

Another way that we can use acts of power to work with resistance is through applying ourselves to an old, one-off goal that we've been avoiding, such as doing our taxes, addressing an issue in our relationship or throwing away all our old, uncomfortable clothes. Acts like these may seem small in comparison with the bigger changes that we can face in our lives, but through working with resistance at this level we can develop the personal power to be free to act no matter how much fear and resistance we're experiencing.

To use this practice, we have to find something that we need to do, but have been putting off for a while. This can be anything you choose, big or small, so long as it feels appropriate to you and the thought of having it done and completed gives you a feeling of relief.

Decide a few days beforehand what you're going to do, and when, and be firm about it. You may like to write down your goal in your journal, tell a friend, or even hold a little ceremony to solidify your intent - whatever you feel will work best for you.

Give yourself the time and space to acknowledge your resistance. There's a reason why it's taken you this long to achieve this goal, and you need to honour that reason before you can move past it. Journal about how you feel about facing this task, or use your time for connecting with the Sacred to pray about the issue, or journey to speak with your guides about it.

When the time that you've chosen comes, be firm but gentle with yourself, knowing that you have the inner power to achieve this goal. Allow yourself to feel any emotions that come up for you, but don't allow them to get in the way of your decision. You might find it helpful to have a medicine object with you, to call on your guides or Spirit for support, or to speak to the part of you that is afraid or upset, telling it that you recognise how it's feeling but that it's now time to move on.

Honour your own courage for doing what is best for you, and make sure you spend a little time afterwards to re-connect and nourish yourself.

Practice: Facing Fear In The Moment - Working with Power Animals

Our daily lives offer us regular opportunities to exercise our courageous hearts, and it's up to us to use them. When you know a friend is talking about you behind your back, or when your children decide to play up when you're feeling ill, or when your partner forgets to post your mother's birthday present - we regularly come up against situations that make us anxious, tense or stressed, all of which are ultimately based in fear.

It's the little moments like these when giving in to our fears and anxieties can be so tempting, that taking responsibility for the choices we make becomes a courageous act of power. And if you really consider it, it's these moments that are the really frightening ones - the challenges to our truth, our peace, our well being or our love that we don't even see coming. And they come so often that if we don't exercise our courage, we can quickly lose ourselves, our integrity and our personal power - leaving us adrift in a world that's constantly changing around us. But by taking these situations as opportunities for growth and empowerment, we can teach ourselves to reach for our most authentic, connected selves in moments of crisis, leaving us better able to deal with whatever life throws at us.

Working with fear in the moment requires mindfulness, intent and, of course, courage. This kind of practice is more of an attitude than a specific skill or exercise; it involves being aware of when we are under stress, and then accessing our courageous selves so that we can listen to our inner knowing and then make inspired, conscious choices that truly reflect our natures; working with, rather than against, our well being.

As you develop your ability to be courageous over time, this practice will naturally develop until you find yourself making more and more authentic choices in your daily life. But there is something that we can do to help ourselves grow this ability - combining the power of medicine objects and power animals for aligning our intent with our actions and the wider world.

A power animal is a spiritual ally that represents part of our power or 'medicine' - the unique gifts and expressions of Spirit that we have as individual souls. When we work with power animals, we are working directly with the essence of that medicine, so that we can develop a deeper and more lasting relationship with it in our lives. We can meet and work with power animals in the same way we met and worked with our guides - through the shamanic journey.

To meet your courage power animal and begin to work with them, choose a time when you won't be disturbed and create a sacred space. Ask for the Sacred to join you, and communicate your intent for the journey, asking for a power animal who can guide you and teach you about courage to meet you at your place in the Spirit World.

Begin to journey in the way that works best for you, using drumming, movement, singing or silence. When you reach the spirit world, call for your guides to join you, and tell them your intent again - that you want to meet a power animal for working with courage. Look around and be open to whatever creature comes to you - the animal who is going to teach you about courage might be very different from what you expect!

When an animal does appear, greet them and ask if they're your courage power animal. If they say yes, you can begin to work with them, asking them what they'd like to be called, how they want to work with you and what gifts or teachings they bring with them.

You may find that they want you to create an altar, or a medicine object, so that they can work with you more directly in the physical world. Or they may teach you a 'courage song' or a prayer to use when you want to access your courageous aspects. You relationship with them and the work you do together will be unique to you - so long as it feels true and right, go with it and trust yourself.

Once you have established the terms of your relationships, thank them and your guides for coming to work with you, and return to the everyday world. Ground yourself as usual, closing sacred space with gratitude and respect, and then make sure that you write down everything that happened in your journal. And, of course, ensure that you do whatever you agreed with your new power animal, so that your relationship gets off to a good start.

Now that you've got a connection to your power animal, you can begin to work with it 'in the moment', calling on it's medicine to help you be courageous and authentic. Develop your own ways of working with this powerful ally, like wearing a handmade totem round your neck or writing a unique prayer that calls on your animal, and saying it when you feel challenged.

Get familiar with the teachings and gifts of your power animal. Each one is different, and will be different depending on who's working with them too. For example, an eagle power animal could be about being able to fly above the issue and see the bigger picture, or about being able to swoop down and take what you need decisively and without hesitation. It all depends on you and your unique expression of courage and power that this animal has come to teach you about.

Practice: Working With Support

As well as working with power animals, there are other strategies that we can use to support ourselves and our efforts to be courageous. We all deserve all the help that we can get when we're striving for more well being, empowerment and peace, and while it's sometimes tempting to 'go it alone', asking for help and support can in fact be a powerful practice in developing courage.

It can be daunting to reveal our vulnerabilities or fears to others, or even to admit them to ourselves. But when we're able to ask for help and guidance, we're actually facing that fear of betrayal, disappointment or embarrassment, which can in turn help us to grow our courage as well as to develop the support strategies that will help us when courage is truly needed.

Practising asking for support can take many forms. It could mean having a compassionate chat with your partner about something that's worrying you, or asking for Spirit to guide you through a particular situation in the best way possible. Sometimes, it can be simply admitting that we need some kind of help, even just to ourselves, and then being open to however that help presents itself, and at other times it can be about being open and honest with the people around us about what the actual situation is, and the support we need to resolve it.

Support can also be about having strategies and tools for supporting ourselves in using our courage when it's most needed, such as when we use prayer, opening sacred space, going for a walk in nature, or meeting with a support group to help us keep calm, connected and clear about what the best action is for us.

As a beginning practice in support, try to ask for help at least once a week. Be clear about what it is you're asking for, and listen to your inner truth about what you really need. You could ask a colleague for help with your work load, a stranger for help with directions, your children for help with any household chores, or anything else that feels appropriate and helpful for you as part of your everyday life. Recognise any resistance you have to asking for support, and acknowledge that part of you for its care and desire to keep you safe. Be firm with yourself, but also be gentle, and know that we are our own most powerful and reliable source of support, so long as we trust ourselves enough to ask.

Section Five:

Vision

We are what we think. All that we are arises with our thoughts.
With our thoughts, we make the world.
Buddha

Vision is our power to see, not just what is, but what could be. With it, we experience all the levels of reality around us, from the physical, material and definite to the potential, the spiritual and energetic. When we journey, day dream or meditate, or visualize healing, we are using our Vision - our ability to see not just with our physical eyes but with our hearts, our minds and our energies. The 'seeing' that we experience in this way isn't just visual, but goes beyond any single sense, and is most often described as direct experience, intense feeling or simple knowing.

Our power of Vision allows us to decipher the world around us, fitting it into our maps of what is true, what is real, what is important and what is useful to us. Without it, we couldn't understand our lives in any meaningful way - we would be lost, blind to all but the most material reality of our existence.

When we are able to use Vision, we can see the opportunities, significances, gifts, signs and blessings of the events that are unfolding around us. We can imagine how each choice may turn out, and the situations that we'd most like to experience. And we can shift our perception of the whole of our lives, calling another focus into our experience and so engaging change and using it to our advantage.

Because of this, developing our ability to see clearly and truly is vital if we want to become more comfortable with change and with life in general. If we don't use our power of vision, we remain unable to interact with the changes around us - we can't move beyond experiencing life as a river that carries us, rather than being the river itself, choosing its path as it flows.

Growing our ability to see, and to envision the world around us, is like any other power that we've explored in this book - it depends on our willingness to try new things, to practice and be open to our greater abilities. When we can do this, suspending our disbelief and allowing our vision to show us new facets of our lives, we can move forward into partnership with the rest of the world, working together to create a rich and beautiful tapestry of life that we have co-created.

All of the personal powers we have developed in this book are interwoven with each other - connection allows us to find our truth, truth allows us to see clearly and develop our relationship with the sacred, our vision allows us to understand and practically apply our connection, and our courage allows us to move forward with all of these powers, to grow, despite any fears and doubts we may have.

And by developing Vision in an effective, harmonious way uses all of the other powers we've worked on. By grounding our Vision in our spiritual connection, we learn to see joyfully, compassionately and in harmony with the rest of creation. When we see from a place of personal truth, our Vision becomes deeper, more unique and personal to us, and free of any misconceptions or restrains that don't belong to us. And when we are able to bring our courageous selves to our dreaming, we can let ourselves see with passion, and power, free to really see what will nourish our souls the most and help us to thrive.

And, like all the other powers, Vision is developed through practising it in our real, day to day lives so that we become comfortable and skilful at applying it when we need it most.

Fundamental Vision Practices

When we first learn about Vision, it can seem strange. How can seeing something that's not 'real' have any power or be useful for us? When we're in school, we're taught that daydreaming is a waste of time, and when we want to discount something, we tell ourselves that it's 'all in our imagination'. But when we take this attitude, we're wasting a huge part of our potential, as well as our personal power.

Our ability to imagine, to envision and to perceive beyond the constraints of our physical senses is a part of what makes us human, and it allows us to be creative, to experience the deeper layers of meaning that life has, and to use opportunities that only we can see.

To learn how to use our Vision, we first have to discover the power and beauty of our imaginations and our inner vision - the images and sensations that we experience in dreams, visualisations, when we're reading books and when we're planning for the future. The exact images and sensations, in fact, that are often discounted as just 'in our heads'.

Developing our ability to envision is about learning to see and perceive with our minds and our hearts, rather than just our physical eyes. We can do this by practising those things that create these kinds of perceptions - daydreaming, visualising, shamanic journeying, imagining and working with our energy.

Practice: Daydreaming, Visualising and Imagining

...the imagination is integral to the processes of creation...
Ly de Angeles

To begin to work with our inner Vision, we need to become familiar with what it feels like. This is an ability that almost all of us use on a regular basis, without even thinking about it. But, like other unconscious abilities, when we try to use it we can get confused and unsure of ourselves.

The best way to get over this is to practice using our inner vision on a daily basis, through daydreaming, visualising and imagining. You can fit these practices into your daily connection routine, or simply do them briefly throughout the day - the point is that you use your inner perception and pay attention to what it feels like, how it works for you, and which methods are best.

Daydream about anything you like, whatever comes to mind and feels comfortable and appropriate to you. You may find it helpful to do your visualisation practice just before you go to sleep, or when you wake up in the morning, as this can be when we're most mentally relaxed and open. The most important thing to remember is to focus on topics that feel right to you, and that leave you feeling happy and full of well being.

Obviously, don't practice using your inner vision when you need to focus on your physical senses - like when you're driving!

Practice: Journeying For Vision

Another good practice that develops our inner Vision is shamanic journeying. When we journey to the Spirit World, we use our imaginations to 'paint' the canvas of energy that exists all around us, overlaying it with a familiar map so that we can interact with it in a way we understand.

The more we journey, the more our Vision will develop. Integrating this practice into your daily routine for a month can very quickly help you to become confident in your inner perception and how you uniquely experience your power of Vision.

It's important to remember when journeying that Inner Vision doesn't have to be visual - we can feel, smell, hear, see and even just sense in a way that goes beyond our physical definitions of sensation, because we are perceiving with our energy, rather than our bodies.

The same goes for all of the Vision practices - don't feel worried if you aren't 'seeing' something, or don't see clearly. Allow your own unique way of perceiving to develop, and be open to all the ways in which you are sensing and seeing, rather than assuming that you should be experiencing your journey a certain way.

You might like to journey for specific guidance on your Vision. For example, you could ask your guides to teach you a specific method for seeing clearly, or ask to meet a power animal who can work with you on this personal power.

As before, just remember that it's how you feel about your practice that matters the most, so pay attention to your inner truth as you do this practice, and listen to what it's telling you.

Practice: Experiencing Our Energetic Vision

The final practice we're going to look at when we start working with Vision is an energetic one. Working directly with energy is wholly dependant on our inner vision, so it's a good practice for developing this personal power. It will also help you to consciously control this ability, keeping your boundaries clear and strong so that you don't end up 'seeing' all sorts of things that you shouldn't!

To do this practice, you first need to decide on a few places to work with, because you're going to be experimenting with the energy of place. Think about places that you can easily get to, and come up with a list of four that are distinctly different from each other; a familiar place, a relatively strange place to you, a busy or well-populated place, and a place that usually has less people moving through it would all be good places to work with. You're looking to experience the contrast between these places, which is why it's helpful for them to be quite different from each other. Let your decision come to you over the space of a few days, or you could even ask to be guided to a particular place by your spirit guides or power animals if that appeals to you.

Once you have decided on the places you're going to work with, set aside some time over the coming weeks to visit them and just spend some time there with no other pressures or focus besides experiencing your vision. Take a few minutes when you arrive to settle into the space, and then open sacred space around you with your favourite method for calling on Spirit and connecting.

Once you can feel that sense of connection and sacredness around you, tell Spirit and your guides what you intend to do here and then begin to turn your focus to the space around you. What can you feel from within your bubble of sacred space? Notice all of the sensations, thoughts, images, sounds and knowings that come up for you, whether internal or external.

You will find that simply by being in sacred space, your awareness of the space is changed, and your ability to directly perceive the energy around you is enhanced. Allow this extra sensitivity to inform you of all the subtleties of the place; you may find that your perception of it now is different to when you were just there in your day to day life, or that you understand why you've always felt a certain way about this space but could never put your finger on why.

Take some notes about your experience and then close sacred space with thanks to Spirit and your guides for safely holding you while you were opening up to the energies around you. Know that as you close sacred space, you are also ending your practice and closing down your sensitivity to spiritual energies, so that you can go back to your day without being affected by any energies elsewhere.

Try this practice at each of your four locations, noticing the differences and similarities between the energies of each space, as well as how your vision manifests for you individually – do you primarily see, or hear or simply 'know' how the energy is? Is it a subtle overlaying of sensation over the external environment, or a clear internal picture, or possibly an enhancement of certain details and sensations beyond their physically normal range?

You may find that you have actually been seeing and experiencing the world around you like this for a long time, and that now you're conscious of what you're doing you have more control about the perceptions and energies you allow into your experience. It may make sense of past experiences of discomfort or resonance with certain people and places – you may recognise specific energies that you've come into contact with before but never realised what they actually were. Or the practice may simply and gently open you up to a whole new layer of perception about the world around you.

Seeing Joyfully and Freely

One of the most important things that we need to remember when we're practising our power of vision is to pay attention to how we feel. Vision that comes from our connection will be joyful, peaceful and clear - reflecting the truth of our relationship with the Sacred.

But if we try to envision from a place of disconnection – a place of fear - we see the world in a painful, frightening or constrictive light. This is because disconnection leaves us, and our perspective, incomplete; we cannot see all that is relevant in the situation, we may resort to 'thinking' rather than seeing, and our own personal wounds and issues will be reflected back to us in our perception.

This is why the first and most important practice we can use for developing our Vision is connection. When we have a strong connection and are comfortable in our relationship with the Sacred, our Vision will come naturally from that place within us, and it will be helpful and nourishing for us. Our envisioning will be tempered with compassion, as we sense the interrelatedness of all life around us, and we will be lead in our co-creation not by what we think we want, but by what is truly best for us and everyone around us.

Connecting as we envision also allows us to access our inner knowing or truth as we see the world around us - making what we are seeing personally relevant to us, practical in our own lives and grounded in our experience. When our vision stems from our inner truth, based on personal experience and feeling, it becomes not just nourishing, but harmonious with the rest of creation - allowing us to participate in the changes around us alongside the Sacred, rather than against it. It becomes grounded in reality, rather than fantasy.

And Vision also requires our courage, which can be found

through our connection as well. Courage allows us to see freely, reaching for the most beautiful perception of our lives that we dare to hold, instead of settling for the vision that everyone else has of us and the world. When we bring our courage to our dreaming practices, we open ourselves up to the possible and the potential, rather than just the probable.

By practising our ability to see alongside our practices of connection, truth and courage, we develop our vision in the most helpful way. Working with these four powers together, we become able to see life and ourselves in a way that not just serves us, but everyone and everything around us too.

And when we practice in this way, our vision becomes the way that we can actively take part in the changes that go on around us - helping us to create maps of life that lead us where we truly want to go, and sourcing these maps from the heart of Spirit, where the highest good for all beings is possible and achievable.

Participating in change from this perspective means that we can confidently effect change around us, in the knowledge that we are working in harmony with the rest of creation, rather than against it. It also means that, as we work to effect the changes we envision, we are supported by the rest of creation - sometimes in the most surprising and magical ways imaginable!

Practice: Grounding Vision Within Our Sacred Connection

It's only when we experience our connection to infinity that
we're able to dream powerfully.
Alberto Villoldo, Courageous Dreaming

To ground and integrate our power of vision within our connection, it can be really helpful to use the ancient practice of working with medicine objects. To do this practice you will need a small stone, either raw or carved, that resonates for you and can represent your power of vision. You may find that you already have the right object, or that one comes to you as you consider performing this practice, or you may even like to specifically go and out find or craft the object with this practice in mind – whatever feels best for you and fits with how you like to work.

Once you have this object, you can empower it as your Vision Stone through ceremony and shamanic journeying. The exact method you choose will depend on how comfortable you are with the various techniques and practices you've learned, as well as what feels most appropriate at this point for this practice.

The fundamental method for empowering your Vision Stone will be to open sacred space, telling Spirit and your guides of your intent, as well as explaining what you intend to the stone itself. Then, you will either call up within you the essence of your power of vision, or journey to retrieve this essence from the spiritual realm, and then blow it into your stone.

By doing this in sacred space and with the support of Spirit you are accessing the most essential expression of your power of vision, the purest and most connected version of this power, and then grounding it into the physical world and your life by bringing it through into a material object.

This is a very powerful and sacred practice that will allow you to always access your most connected, sacred vision, and I would recommend that you spend the time to craft a really beautiful ceremony to contain this work so that you get the most from it.

Once you have empowered your Vision Stone, you can work with it in the way that you work with any other medicine objects – through wearing it, putting it on an altar, journalling with it and spending time with it. You can also call on its medicine specifically when you're practising and using your power of vision, so that you always source from your deepest connection with the sacred when you do this work.

Practice: Becoming Self Referencing

Once we are able to see from a place of sacred connection, we can begin to access our truth when dreaming.

To see freely, we must be able to choose for ourselves - to listen to our own truth, and to see from our own, authentic perspective, without fear. If we aren't free, our Vision is clouded and restricted, leaving us only able to create situations that come from other people, or that only half-meet our needs.

Seeing freely means that we have to be self referencing; perceiving directly from the resources we have within us - our truth, our connection, our courage and our experiences. Becoming self referencing is a process that calls on all of our power to be courageous; while not for the faint hearted, it is a hugely empowering achievement that grows continuously as we do.

To do this, we simply have to bring our mindfulness to what we are seeing, allowing our truth to speak through us and listening to it instead of ignoring it. An excellent practice to support this process is journalling. When we write down our thoughts, feelings, visions and ideas, we are totally alone with them. We have the space to unravel and examine them properly, tracking them to their sources.

The most important question to answer when you are journalling to become self referencing is - what would I know about this if I could only count on my direct, personal experience? Discount any hearsay, conjecture, rumours or teaching that you haven't experienced first-hand. Discard what others have told you. Look at every belief you hold about the situation, and check that each one is based on actual experience.

It is amazing how this exercise can shift your perception - opening up whole new possibilities that were otherwise assumed to be impossible, or were even simply invisible to your awareness.

Each of these practices requires and develops our courage, as well as our ability to connect with the Sacred and to know the truth that lives within us. Bringing these personal powers to our Vision is hugely empowering for us, not only for developing our ability to perceive more joyfully, clearly and freely, but also enhancing all of our other powers for thriving in change.

Applying Vision In Our Lives

Once we are comfortable with using our Vision from a place of connection and truth, we can begin to apply this power in our lives. Using Vision in daily life, like all other practices, develops and grows our Vision, as well as being a tool for thriving during change - through using it, it becomes stronger, and we become more trusting of it, which makes it more and more effective for us.

Applying Vision in our lives simply requires that we use it, coming from a place of connection and authenticity. Every time that we imagine our intended outcome when we make a decision, every time we daydream about a goal we're reaching for, and each time that we explore the situation we're in from more than just a physical perspective, we are using our power of Vision in a practical way.

But just like the other powers we've explored, Vision can also be applied consciously, as part of our journey towards becoming more comfortable with change.

Practice: Vision As Part Of Our Daily Connection

One way that we can consciously apply our power of Vision is to integrate it into our daily connection practices. This is often a very simple and effective way of developing our Vision while at the same time benefiting from it's power to bring about change in our lives mindfully and actively.

The effects of our vision practice are often very subtle, commonly taking place over months and years rather than days, and so applying this practice regularly, and in small, comfortable amounts, allows us to cumulatively build this ability and the changes it brings to our lives.

One way to begin integrating our Vision into our connection practice is through visualisation - by seeing in our minds the energies and Spirits that we are working with, we strengthen both our connection to them and our understanding of how that connection works, as well as becoming more confident in our ability to see clearly and accurately. This confidence then carries over into other areas of our dreaming, such as when we visualise outcomes, connect to our bigger dreams and align ourselves with our soul's well being throughout the day.

To use visualisation as a practice, we simply have to become conscious of it as we use it. Almost all of us will already be using visualisation as part of our work with the Sacred, either through visual meditations, journeying, energy work, prayer or just through imagining what we're calling as we open Sacred space. It's a very natural way for many of us to work, and can span across not only seeing but also hearing and feeling.

If you're already doing one of these visualisation practices, then simply become aware of the way you apply your Vision as you do the practice everyday. Notice what and how you see - do you see visually, or is it more of a feeling? Are the images clear, or do they swim into one another? Do you see in colour, is there movement, or is what you see still, like a photograph? If you feel or hear, how much detail do you receive? What kind of sensations do you experience, and where on your body? What happens when you change something in the practice?

Becoming aware of how you are already using your Vision will mean that when you use it to purposefully craft visions of change, or dreams, you'll be able to trust it, and enjoy the process.

If you haven't been using one of the visualisation practices above, or you'd like to try a new one, then a very simple practice is to simply imagine a room in your house in great detail. See it as though you are standing within in it physically, and notice every detail around you. You can focus in on specific objects, or touch things, so that you develop not just your ability to see but also to feel and touch and hear and even smell.

Practising this simple technique on a regular basis will quickly develop the clarity and solidity of your Vision, which will in turn make any other practices that you do that rely on your ability to envision, such as journeying, much more clear and easy to access.

When you practice in this way, it can help to think of your Vision as a skill that you're honing. By developing the focus and awareness that these practices help with, you're strengthening your metaphorical 'seeing muscles' so that you can better use them for the more complex practices that will help you to thrive during change.

Practice: Dreaming and the Law of Attraction

All that is born, all that is created, all the elements of nature are interwoven and united with each other.

Jesus of Nazareth

Dreaming is both a practice in developing Vision, and one of the ways that we can use our Vision to participate in change. Many spiritual traditions and shamanic cultures speak of 'dreaming' or the Law of Attraction in one way or another; the power that we have to create our experiences through changing how we see and perceive the world. In my tradition, we are taught methods for 'dreaming the world into being'; methods that focus not on changing the world around us, but on changing ourselves internally and then allowing those changes to be reflected back to us in our experiences.

This can sound very strange in the context of a materially focused, scientific-minded society, but it's based in concrete and practical observations of how the world works. How many of us have known people who habitually imagine unpleasant situations, and who also constantly meet with such unfortunate situations much more frequently that could possibly be by chance?

And conversely, have you ever known someone who had a glow or sense of grace about them? Someone who always saw the best in everything that they encountered, and who seemed to turn even the worst circumstances into something beautiful and healing?

These are just the extremes of how our perceptions affect how the world around us. Our perceptions and attitudes can impact everything in our lives, including our health, pain levels, wealth and success - if we can't see the beauty and joy in the world around us, we simply can't access it. Which is why the ability to see truly and compassionately is such a powerful gift to develop.

Dreaming focuses on developing this power and then using it consciously to craft our lives. It works through sourcing our perceptions from our powers of connection and truth, and so anchoring them in their most helpful, truthful perspectives. This in turn allows us to see and so to choose to express our highest potential in our lives.

This shifting of the world around us as we shift internally is because of the way that we are connected to the fabric of creation; our personal energies, the most fundamental material that we are made of, are interconnected and interwoven with the energies of everything else in existence. This means that as our energies shift the other energies also change; we are part of creation, and when one part moves, so does the whole.

What this means for us in our daily lives is that each and every experience is created through our interaction with the web of energy around us, and that through shifting our perception, we are transforming the parts of ourselves that have pulled these experiences into our lives, and are opening ourselves up for different energies and experiences instead.

Practising dreaming and working with the law of attraction is a very powerful way to develop our vision, and in turn become comfortable with change. Fundamentally, this practice means being conscious of what we're perceiving and dreaming as we go about our day – by bringing all of these tiny ways that we create our reality into our consciousness, we become aware of just how much power we have over our experiences and we develop the skill of choosing what to attract to us through our power of perception.

Along with mindfulness about our daily perceptions and how we feel about them, we can consciously use dreaming as we go about our day to day life, both to strengthen our skills and to actively engage with change.

Practice: Finding the Feeling

Dreaming is all about the feeling, rather than the thoughts we're thinking. Noticing our feelings, which are so intimately connected with our power of Vision, can tell us exactly what we're focusing on with much greater accuracy than simply being aware of our thoughts. How many of us have had the experience of trying to 'think positively' about a situation that we were really upset about? This isn't dreaming or using the power of our vision, it's denial, and it actually reinforces the energies that we're trying to override rather than attracting new, more positive ones to us!

This is because while our minds can play words games, for example by thinking 'I'm going to win this time', our actual focus is still on how much we want to win, what will happen if we don't, how impossible or improbably it is that we actually will, and how we're never won before. Our thoughts may be turned in the right direction, but our overall awareness is still turned towards the outcome we don't want – our lack of winning. And our feelings will very honestly let us know that this is what's going on!

So when we begin to use the practice of dreaming, it's important to focus more on how we're feeling about the subject we're focusing on, rather than our specific thoughts. And we can use this to our advantage by 'sourcing' a feeling that we're calling into our lives, and then aligning ourselves with that feeling whenever we feel pulled into a different, less helpful focus.

To do this, all we need to do is use our power of Vision. In the same way that many of us daydream or visualise great feeling situations when we're got a free moment, going over and over something because it makes us feel good somehow, we can craft visions in our mind that give us that good feeling we're looking for.

It's good to begin this practice, at least at first, within sacred space, with the support of your guides. Let them know what you're doing, and ask for their help in turning your focus towards the appropriate images and feelings for your intent. You might find it helpful to use memories that create the same feeling as the one you're looking for, or to find pictures or music that nourish that feeling within you. Or you may find that simply by calling for and then being open to the feeling, you begin to feel it growing within you until you are familiar enough with it to recognise and work with it.

However you do it, just remember that you're working with energy and Spirit here, so there's no way to force it – simply open up and allow the feeling to come, trusting that you'll know it when you experience it. And remember to keep it playful; if you become too serious, or start off with something that's too important to you emotionally, your mind is almost bound to get in the way and start veering your focus off onto the opposite of the feeling you're looking for – the lack of what you want to feel, rather than the feeling itself.

Once you have this feeling, you can use it throughout your day to continue to attract the circumstances that will grow and nourish that feeling, whatever they may be. Simply by aligning yourself with this feeling on a regular basis, you will begin to shift the focus and direction of your energy, and so the external world around you will begin to shift as well.

Try to notice how this works for you – we all manifest differently, and each shift will come about in a unique way. It may simply be an internal change, for example a situation that bothered you before becomes easy to handle, or there may be physical changes as well, such as the healing of an old illness, people changing their behaviour towards you, or unexpected synchronicities that bring just what you need into your life.

By focusing on the feeling rather than how you think you can get that feeling, you leave it up to Spirit to decide on the exact how and when of the physical expression of your focus, which can lead to surprising and even miraculous results!

Practice: Choosing Our Focus

Once you've experienced how you can find and align with a feeling throughout your day, you can begin to play with how to affect your life by simply shifting your focus.

Use your new ability to choose a feeling that you want to experience in your day, and set that as your focus. Then see what happens and prepare to be surprised! When we do this, we begin to develop trust in the process of dreaming, allowing us to build up our practice until we can use it for shifting any situation that we're challenged by or want to change.

Just like at the beginning of this chapter when we worked on noticing new things, you need to keep your eyes open for just how these changes will appear to you. The less we put limits on 'how' things might change, the greater potential for true grace and healing will be, so keep focusing on the feeling that you're looking for and let Spirit work out the details.

As a preparation for our next practice, I'd recommend working on 5 or 10 dreaming projects in this way to build up your familiarity with the process and your trust in the way Spirit works with you when you dream. Allow yourself lots of time for these projects to manifest – the less limitations or pressures that you put on this work at the beginning, the more success you will have as there will be less chance of your mind interfering and getting stressed about it.

Start small – simply focus on experiencing a slightly higher energy for a day, or having a positive encounter with someone you often rub the wrong way. Focus on how it will feel to to experience these things, and allow that feeling to grow within you without any pressure on the outcome – as if you were simply doing an experiment in the power of your Vision.

Once you're comfortable with these more subjective shifts in your experience, you can begin to dream up bigger changes. Perhaps you'd like a new writing pen? Or you need a particular resource for a craft project or a new piece of furniture? Find how having these things would feel for you, disregarding any thoughts about 'how' or 'when' you could get them, and then spend some time regularly focusing on that feeling and see what happens.

When I've done this, the objects or experiences I've been looking for have turned up in the most surprising ways, and sometimes in very normal, mundane ways – I've found the piece of furniture I needed in a charity shop for a tenth of what it would cost new, or the piece of wood for my carving in the skip. Or someone just happens to have a pen they don't want any-more, and would I like it?

Once you begin to trust your dreaming and relax into the process so that there's no pressure or negative focus involved, these kinds of things happen on a regular basis.

Try working in this way for a good few months, slowly building up your comfort with dreaming and your own ways of working with it. You may find that integrating your dreaming into your daily spiritual routine works for you, or that you work best when you simply bring up the feeling within you at points throughout your day. You might like to create a dreaming board, with images and quotes that illicit the feeling you're looking for, or that drawing, writing or simply daydreaming works for you.

And remember to note down your experiences in your journal

– it can be very easy for our minds to jump in after the experience, to downplay or rationalise away what happened. It's important that we remain aware of the miracles that we're calling into our lives, and our own part in creating them, and a record of our experiences that we can occasionally look over is invaluable for this, especially when we're challenged with a particularly uncomfortable change in our lives and need to remember our power.

Practice: Sourcing your BIG Dream

I say, you want to change? Then do not, under any circumstances, allow yourself to settle on a vision or a calling or a change in any arena that is uninspiring. If you're going to have clarity on something in your life, make it something so big and bright and meaningful that you will get out of bed and chase it until you grasp it or die. Bring forth a desire that knows no safe boundaries and even scares you a little bit, that will demand all the best that is in you, that takes you out of your own orbit and into the stratosphere of the remarkable. That kind of desire changes your life, and it changes the world.
Brendon Burchard, The Charge

When we try to control the small details in our lives, we end up micromanaging rather than envisioning, or dreaming, our lives into being - forcing things to fit into what we think 'should' be happening, rather than allowing events to naturally unfold around us from the source of our inner connection. Creating our lives from a place of vision is easy and effortless as we step from one situation to the next, whereas forcing and managing our lives to fit a certain ideal is exhausting, frustrating and ultimately disappointing as the myriad of forces and patterns of creation around us break out of our rigidly held mould and appear to get in our way. When we slip into micromanaging our lives with our heads rather than dreaming them with our hearts and souls, we end up burning out and getting disillusioned.

A great antidote to this is to find our big dream - the dream that's too big to even begin thinking about, the one that we can only 'feel' about instead. Our big dream fills up our hearts and brings us out of the mental, 'is it possible?' perspective and into a place of soulful vision, potentiality, and flow.

Our big dreams come from our souls, the place where we are uniquely and intimately connected with Spirit. When you find yours, it will seem to flow through you from that deep, unknown place; filling you with passion and energy and renewed purpose. And when you live your big dream, vision stops being about getting what you want, and becomes your way of being - you can't help but see the beauty and purpose in your life, and everything slots into place within the process of creating your vision.

To discover our big dream, we have to source it. Similar to any of work of creation, it cannot be reasoned or thought into being, but must be allowed to flow through us when the time is right. But there are ways that we can encourage this knowledge of our soul's purpose to become conscious, and once again we return to the power of ceremony for calling up and creating that which goes beyond mind and words.

For calling up and discovering your big dream, you could use many of the ceremonies described in this book, from Despachos to Fire ceremonies depending on what you're drawn to. The important factor in guiding your ceremony will be your intent - being clear about why you're holding the ceremony, and what you want to gain from it, is vital to its success. This ceremony isn't about creating or even being able to fully envision your big dream, but about discovering where it lies within you so that you can begin to build a relationship with it. You have to be able to feel your dream somewhere in your awareness to begin uncovering it within your life and aligning your energy with it.

I'm not going to give you a ceremony for this. Instead, I'm

going to encourage you to create one for yourself. By now you'll have enough of a feel for your own spiritual expression, as well as a solid base of ceremonial experience, to know what works for you and what doesn't. Follow your heart and allow it to guide you - you are the best judge of what you need.

You could begin with a ceremonial form that we've already touched on, like the fire ceremony or altar work, and build from that, or you could make something up that's all yours - do whatever you're most comfortable with. Simply remember the fundamental elements of ceremony - connection with the Sacred, symbolism and intent.

Bring these three elements together in your own unique way, seeing how it will look and feel as you do the ceremony and trusting any specific details that come to you as you envision how your ceremony will unfold. There are so many variations and possibilities that you can draw from, so this is a great practice in itself for focusing your vision as you listen to your inner knowing and connection in order create something that is uniquely nourishing and helpful for you.

Doing this ceremony will call up within you a big dream, one that is rooted in your deepest nature and will guide you on your journey of growth and exploration. Like when we work with other ceremonies, the results can be dramatic or subtle, fast or slow, expected or surprising, depending on where we are in our lives and what we're ready for. The most important thing to remember is to stay open and aware, and to keep practising your connection regularly so that when you begin to feel your big dream and what it might be, you have the time and the support to focus on and recognise it.

This dream could be anything, and the more open-minded we are about what it could be, the more beneficial this work will be for us. Often, what our minds think we want, or should be doing, is very different from what our souls need. It could be that we think we need more money, when our souls really feel that we need more nourishing time out of doors, or that we believe we have to use one particular gift that we've got, when our souls know that developing another, more rewarding talent will be better for us and everyone around us in the long run.

As time goes on after this ceremony, you may find yourself noticing how you're feeling about one area of your life or another. Something new might catch your eye, or you might become re-connected to an old passion - it's all possible, and will be totally unique to you. So let it happen, and keep journalling as you keep your eyes open for the big dream that is calling to you right now.

Practice: Aligning With Your BIG Dream

Once you are more aware of what your big dream is and how it feels, you can start to work with it in your day to day life. Aligning with your big dream means focusing on the things that match up with your dream as you go through your day - allowing yourself to become more and more aware of that feeling of passion and clarity, and letting it grow in your life.

Through doing your Big Dream ceremony, you may have a good idea of what your dream is and what it looks like, or you might simply have a feeling, a passing insight into how you want to feel in your life. Either is fine, because what we focus on most of all when we're working with vision as part of our lives, is not details but feelings and emotions.

This is because, if we try to focus on specific images or ideas and then cling to them in our vision there is no room for growth, and our dream can become stuck and lifeless - unable to change as we do, or to reveal the various levels of meaning it holds for us.

For example, through your Big Dream ceremony and journalling work you many have discovered the vision of a beautiful home living within you. This is a wonderful dream to have, and through working with it in our daily lives we can begin to create that vision so that we experience it in our lives.

However, if we focus on a fixed image, possibly the initial image we discovered while looking for our Big Dream, or another image that we decided on as we thought about our dream, we begin to limit that process of creation. We close off doors that might lead to something that would feel just as good, and that would meet the terms of the dream that our soul is dreaming, because it doesn't fit our specific image of what our dream should look like. And the more detailed the image that we're holding as 'the dream' we want to create, the more we limit our creativity and any opportunities for the rest of the universe to respond to our dream and help us out.

Because of this, it's important to keep our focus on the feel and vision of the dream, rather than the details - for the moment. Keeping our vision open like this will mean that we are able to access all the support, opportunities and synchronicity that the world will offer to us.

With this is mind, one of the best practices for aligning with our big dream during the course of our day is mindfulness. When we are aware of how we are feeling and what we are responding to both within and without us, we can begin to 'track' our vision - following the signs and patterns that are all around us, and that act as doorways that we can step through as we create our dream.

We can begin to do this is by consciously setting aside a small amount of time to be mindful, at any point in our day; time where we can focus on noticing how we feel about our lives, and looking at what situations are creating feelings that resonate with our dream, and which situations are creating other, less helpful feelings.

You may find it helpful to journal about what you notice during these periods of mindfulness, asking yourself questions such as - what gave me the best feeling today? What events or objects in my day could symbolise my dream? How did I feel about this experience?

Notice any significant feelings you had, but try to focus on the enjoyable, beautiful feelings the most. Notice what made you feel more connected, soulful and passionate.

Looking at our lives in this way helps us to discover and track down any avenues that might lead us closer to our dream. But the most important reason to use practices like these are that they develop our vision in alignment with our soul's purpose and connection, like turning a search light to face in the direction we want to travel. The more we focus on that direction, the more our momentum and energy will move towards the dreams of our soul.

There are a lot of books and various teachers on the ways that we can use Vision to consciously create what we want in life. The many maps that we can apply to using Vision in our lives come with many names, from the Law of Attraction to Conscious Dreaming, and I would recommend that you explore any and all of these methods that call to you. Our power of Vision is a mysterious and personal thing, and just like all of the other powers that we're working with here, it works best when we've thoroughly explored and connected to it on a personal level, understanding how and why it works for us, and how best to work with it in our lives.

Letting Go

The final stage of dreaming our lives is letting it all go. As you have no doubt found out for yourself by now, life and spirit are mysterious, un-knowable things, and we just can't control them, pin them down or 'get' it all in the way that our over-active minds often struggle to do.

Letting it go is what I call the process of surrendering to the Sacred. It requires the courage, trust, faith and personal understanding that comes from a deep connection with the Sacred, and the ability to see the truth of who we really are and how we have been provided for in every moment of our lives.

Letting it go involves stepping back from our vision, stopping our efforts to understand everything and relaxing into where we are now - knowing that the future will take care of itself. Being able to do this is a skill that comes from our inner powers, and by developing your ability to connect, know the truth, exercise courage and see clearly, you will begin to develop your ability to let go and let the Sacred do the work for you.

When we are able to let it all go, we find our ability to be peaceful in any circumstance. This is the peace that religions and all spiritual traditions speak of; knowing who we are as spiritual beings, and how we relate personally to the great sacredness that is all of creation, allows us to ride any storm and flow with any change.

All the work that you have done up to this point - building your personal relationship with Spirit, discovering your own, inner truth, growing your courage and power, and honing your vision - all of this work has been developing your power to let go.

To be able to consciously use this power, we simply have to learn a method that works for us - one that helps us to disconnect from the issue or vision or question or feeling and return to an everyday, peaceful perspective. There are many ways that we can do this, probably one or more for each of us, and the way that works best for you will be as unique as every other practice and experience you have had on this journey. I've included a few of my favourite techniques, and you can find others in almost every spiritual tradition - I encourage you to go and explore as many as you can!

Practice: Gratitude For Now

Dwelling in the present moment, I know that this is a wonderful moment.
Thich Nhat Hanh, Being Peace

We've used gratitude before, as a way to build both connection and trust. It's such a powerful practice that it could form a whole spiritual path all by itself, and if it works for you then gratitude can be a brilliant foundation for your daily spiritual routine.

To use gratitude as a practice in letting go, look for the perfection in what is now. Being appreciative of what you do have and giving sincere thanks for it is a powerful way to accept and let go of your current situation.

It may be that you're feeling stuck, or the other practices you're using don't seem to be helping; you may be calling up all your energy and power to take a new step on your path. Or you might be feeling so focused on the past, or on achieving a specific outcome, that you're blocking yourself from healing and moving forward.

Whatever the situation, if you look for the beauty, joy, truth or power in it, you will find it. And when you're able to find this sacred light inside of where you are right now, you will have let go of all the things that are 'wrong' with your situation - we can only truly focus on one thing at a time, so if you make sure it's all the positives of where you are, the negatives can only fall away.

A great gratitude practice that I've used personally again and again, especially when things have got tough, has been simply to list everything that I'm thankful for in my life at that moment. To use this practice, take a little time to sit with your journal, somewhere you will be undisturbed. For a few moments, simply call to the Sacred and ask it to be with you, using your favourite method for opening sacred space. Take a few deep breaths, and try to allow any tension or upset fall from you as you focus on where you are in that moment.

Write at the top of a page "Right now, I give thanks for...", then allow the things that are positive in your life come into your attention.

Note each one down as it comes, giving thanks as you do, and then move on to the next one. If any unhelpful thoughts come up, just turn your focus back to what you're giving thanks for.

> For example:
> Today, I give thanks for....
> my children
> the kiss my husband gave me this morning
> having enough food in the house for lunch
> having this beautiful house to sleep in tonight
> my hands that are writing this
> my healthy body
> my parents
> the sun coming through the window
> the earth beneath my feet
> being able to share this with you
> a good night's sleep
> my connection with Spirit
> the teachings I've learnt
> the honeysuckle on our studio wall
> the blackbird singing
> the book I'm reading
> the smell of my son's hair

Once you begin to write your list, you might find that you can't stop! Focusing on the positive things we appreciate in our lives opens up our vision to even more of the positive and potentially positive situations in our life, as well as gently detaching our focus from what's wrong, what we lack or what we're trying to create.

Practice: Releasing To Spirit

Another great practice for letting it all go so that we can get on with enjoying our lives is releasing to Spirit.

Releasing to Spirit is a way for us to surrender control of the situation into the hands of our higher selves, our souls, and to the care of the Sacred. It is a way for us to recognise and honour the limited perspective of a human life, and ensure that our own personally limited perspective doesn't get in the way of our well being.

Releasing something to Spirit requires that we symbolically and energetically share responsibility for our lives with the only other being or force that we can - the Sacred. We can do this at the end of our daily routines and dreaming practices, as well as at the end of any ceremonies, and it will help us to get back into our normal, everyday focus.

There are many ways that we can release something to Spirit, or the Sacred. The way that we use will depend on who we are, what our relationship with the Sacred is like, and what it is that we're releasing. The most important factors in releasing something to Spirit are the symbolism we use, and our intent. So long as the action we use is a metaphor for surrender, relinquishment or letting go, it will be an effective vessel for what we're trying to do. And so long as our intent is it to truly let go and let the Sacred deal with the issue for us, trusting that Spirit knows what is best for all beings, then our intent will be effective.

I've included a few of the ways that I've used to release

something to Spirit, many of which are common and obvious. You could use one of these methods, or make up one of your own if that feels more appropriate - remember that this is simply a small ceremony to contain and make real your intent to let go. Just like any other ceremony that you have created from scratch or have modified from someone else's method, it's all about how you feel, the vision you hold and the meaning you give it.

To release the work that you've been doing at the end of your daily spiritual practice, take a moment or two to settle, letting the work you've done really sink in and breathing naturally and comfortably. When you're ready, begin to gather all of those thoughts, feelings and visions that you've been working with.

Call them up inside you, bring them forward through your energy, and see them gathering in front of your body. Notice how they look and feel, using your Vision to perceive them clearly, and knowing that as you imagine them gathering, they will do so easily and quickly.

Once you feel that all of your thoughts and feelings, your ideas and emotions are gathered up, reach out and hold them between your hands. Become aware of how they sit in your palms, noticing the sensations of all that energy.

Now pass them up to Spirit as though you're gently throwing a ball into the air - let the Sacred take all of that energy and thought and feeling, and know that you can get on with your day while Spirit continues the work that you were doing.

Another way to do this is to give your thoughts and visions to a medicine object to hold for you, by blowing into it and asking the Spirit of your medicine object to work with and transform the issue while you go about your day. Tell the Sacred and your medicine object that you'd like them to handle it from now on, for the moment, or until a specific time, so that you can let it go and focus on something else, knowing that the situation is in safe hands.

You could also to write down the situation or vision in your journal and consciously close the book, leaving it in a special place and asking Spirit to take care of it for you until your return. Or you could blow out the candle you were using to hold sacred space, or say a prayer of thanks and release, such a as 'thy will be done'.

Whichever method that you choose to use, simply know that by releasing that issue, situation or vision to Spirit, you are allowing a space to form in your energy and your life. It is in this space that miracles happen, and where the Sacred co-creates with us most powerfully.

Letting go of our path, our work, our vision, our wound or our situation allows us to really focus on where we are right now, in this moment. It returns our life to us afresh, without meaning that we become disconnected from our spiritual connection and power.

By sharing responsibility for what we create in our lives, we can relax. We know that, while we are in a limited perspective because of our physical natures, we can trust the infinite wisdom and compassion of the Sacred and our own Sacred selves to create what's best for us - if we can just relax and let them do it.

So do the practices that you enjoy, live by your dream, listen to your heart and then let it all go and get on with living your life.

Thriving In Change

I will show you until this point only. From there, make it up yourself. You must learn to trust what is inside yourself. You all have very good things inside you.
Masaaki Hatsumi & Benjamin Cole, Understand? Good. Play!

We are all living in a constantly changing world, and we're all constantly changing. Just look back at the work that you've done and how it's changed you as you've read this book – even if you've done none of the practices, there are new thoughts, new ideas and new responses inside you regarding change, the Sacred, ceremony, courage, vision, and what is meant by truth. You've changed.

'You've changed' - we often say that as if it's a bad thing, as if we wish that the world and everyone around us would just stop, hold still, freeze – but is that really what we want? Or do we want the power to flow with the changes around us and make the most of them in our lives, finding peace, enjoyment and opportunity within the shifting world?

For me, the thought of a frozen world, one where nothing moves, no one grows, nothing's born or dies, and where I stay the same person for my whole life sounds terrible. It actually sounds like being dead, not alive.

To be truly alive, we have to change, and we have to let the world change too. This is a beautiful thing, once we get the hang of it - once we find the power within us to thrive in the changing world, and become part of that process of change. Being able to connect to our infinite, unchanging nature through our relationship with the Sacred gives us the first step towards this ability – it allows us to know the stability beneath all the seemingly endless shifting and transformation.

Knowing how to recognise truth, and developing the courage

to do so, then enables us to bridge this sacred connection into our human lives. We know that we can always find the truth of who we are and the world around us, because we have the courage to reference for ourselves, to turn inward to the essential nature of reality when we need a little stable ground, and then to bring forth that stability and knowledge of ourselves into our lives in practical ways.

And finally, remembering our power of vision allows us to actively be a part of the all the change around and within us – seeing what could be, choosing what we'd like to feel, and then allowing all of our courage and connection to flow through us into creating our experiences. Through vision, we step out of the place where change happens to us, and actually become the force for change in our own lives.

Through working with these powers, we develop the fundamental grounding that allows us to approach any change with equanimity and enthusiasm. And the more that we practice and use these powers in the face of real change, the more confident and skilful we become at dancing within the process of transformation.

Practice: Change In The Moment

When you're going through a major change such as a divorce, illness, moving house, having a baby or changing career, the work that you've done to develop your powers of connection, truth, courage and vision will really come into it's own.

Through working with the tools and understanding that you've developed through your practice, you have all that you need to make it through the change, not just surviving but thriving; coming out the other side enlightened, empowered and free to create the next stage of your life's journey.

Think about what you need, and what's worked for you in the past. Have you worked well with creating ceremonies, or do you regularly journey for guidance from spirit guides and power animals? Has an altar helped you in the past with a more minor change? Have you found journalling particularly helpful? Or does simply connecting with the Sacred through nature or community give you the strength and nourishment to remain calm and focused on your vision of the truth of who you are and where you're going with your life?

Work with anything and everything that helps in that moment, and don't think about what other people expect or how anyone else thinks you should be feeling.

Part of the work that we've done throughout this book has been about validating your own experience, and knowing the power of your own truth for healing and creating new life experiences – so trust what you're feeling, wanting, thinking and doing, and know that within the sacred connection that you've grown in your life, you will always know deep down what to do next.

This is especially important if you're going through a life change that's commonly perceived as painful or negative; our culture gives us lots of maps about how we should feel during certain experiences, but it's important to give yourself lots of space to really find out what you think and feel about what's going on, rather than what everyone else thinks and feels.

For example, when someone close to you dies it's very common for the people around you to describe it as a tragedy and to compound your grief with confusion over what you're really feeling. It may actually be that you're feeling relieved, if they died after a long illness, or that you feel peaceful and healed about this change and feel no need to grieve deeply as you have a sense of rightness about what has happened.

Whatever it is that you're feeling, honour it and yourself. And conversely, for positive or 'happy' changes such as having a baby or getting a promotion, take the time to honour how you're actually feeling and be open to all the shades of emotion and perception that you have of this event.

All of these feelings and perceptions, emotions and thoughts that come up for us when we're going through a change are part of who we are in that moment; they reveal to us the deepest wounds, judgements and, conversely, healed places within us. Without change, we may never find these places or have the incentive to heal and integrate them.

And that's the gift of change – not only does it allow us to experience all the vibrancy of being alive, but it gives us the opportunity to grow, heal, and know ourselves more and more fully. By working with change as a gift rather than something to be avoided, we can each become so much more than who we once were – we can become all that we have the potential to be, all that is contained within that sacred space of our connection with Spirit, our truest natures as unique, evolving souls. And we can be free.

Recommended Practices

To connect with the Sacred in any situation:
Creating Sacred Space
Connecting With Nature
Working with Altars
Working with Medicine Objects
Gratitude
Silence and Mindfulness
Community
Journalling

For setting intent and asking for support as you move towards
    your goals:
Creating Ceremonies
Despacho Ceremonies
Fire Ceremonies
Sandpaintings
Asking for Help
Releasing to Spirit

For gathering strength, courage and a new perspective during
    difficult situations:
Creating Sacred Space
Shamanic Journeying
Meeting and Working with Guides
Working with Power Animals
Working with Medicine Objects
Asking for Help

For building personal power for use in daily life:
Shamanic Journeying
Shadow Work

Working with Stones
Acts of Power
Being Self-Referencing
Meeting and Working with Guides
Working with Power Animals
Working with Medicine Objects
Journalling
Silence and Mindfulness

For engaging actively with change in your life:
Daydreaming and Visualisation
Sourcing your Big Dream
Creating Ceremonies
Despacho Ceremonies
Fire Ceremonies
Sandpaintings
Silence and Mindfulness
Releasing to Spirit

References

Fools Crow; Wisdom & Power by Thomas Mails
Council Oak Books LLC, Tulsa, USA

Ibid, Log 77 – quoted in Women of Wisdom: The Journey Of The
    Sacred Feminine Through The Ages by Paula Marvelly
Watkins Publishing, London, UK

Welcome Home: Following Your Souls Journey Home by Sandra
    Ingerman
Harper Collins, New York, USA

Strange Enough, Deep Enough from Riven Inside by Carolyn
    Hillyer
Seventh Wave Music, UK

Call Me By My True Names by Thich Nhat Hanh
Paralax Press, Berkeley, USA

The Eye of the Prophet by Khalil Gibran
Souvenir Press Ltd, London, UK

The Essence of Rumi by John Baldock
Eagle Editions, Ltd, Hertfordshire, UK

Number 12. Not Wanting from the Tao Te Ching: A Book About
    The Way And The Power Of The Way by Lao Tzu – translated
    by Ursula K Le Guin
Shambhala Publications, Inc, Boston, USA

Miracle of Mindfulness by Thich Nhat Hanh
Rider, Random House Ltd, London, UK

When Things Fall Apart: Heart Advice for Difficult Times by
    Pema Chödrön
Shambhala Classics, USA

The Places That Scare You: A Guide to Fearlessness in Difficult
    Times by Pema Chödrön
Shambhala Classics, USA

Courageous Dreaming by Alberto Villoldo
Hay House, Inc, USA

Understand? Good. Play! By Masaaki Hatsumi & Benjamin Cole
Bushin Books, USA

Witchcraft: Theory & Practice by Ly de Angeles
Llewellyn Worldwide, Ltd, St Paul, USA

The Gospel of Mary Magdalene, translated by Jean-Yves Leloup
Inner Traditions Bear and Company, USA

Being Peace by Thich Nhat Hanh
Rider, Random House UK Ltd, London, UK

"Still point of the turning world" quote is from Four Quartets 1:
    Burnt Norton by T.S. Eliot

Further Reading & Resources

Dark Side of the Light Chasers: Reclaiming Your Power, Creativity, Brilliance and Dreams by Debbie Ford

Shamanic Journeying: A Beginner's Guide by Sandra Ingerman

Ask And It Is Given: Learning To Manifest The Law Of Attraction by Esther and Jerry Hicks

www.brendonburchard.com

www.seventhwavemusic.co.uk

www.thelivingsacred.org

About the Author

Luitha K Tamaya is an author, teacher and contemporary shaman whose work with Spirit & her guides goes back over 15 years.

She began her formal shamanic training after witnessing her fathers death, using spiritual teachings to recover from and transcend the breakdown that followed.

Now, her passion is teaching these ancient spiritual tools in ways that help real people who are living with real, modern-world, problems.

She lives in Suffolk, UK, with her husband, the artist Gabriel Tamaya, and their family.

You can find out more about how spiritual teachings and tools can be applied to modern life at her website: www.lktamaya.co.uk

AXIS MUNDI
BOOKS

Axis Mundi Books provide the most revealing and coherent explorations and investigations of the world of hidden or forbidden knowledge. Take a fascinating journey into the realm of Esoteric Mysteries, Magic, Mysticism, Angels, Cosmology, Alchemy, Gnosticism, Theosophy, Kabbalah, Secret Societies and Religions, Symbolism, Quantum Theory, Apocalyptic Mythology, Holy Grail and Alternative Views of Mainstream Religion.